Magnolias Without Moonlight

Magnolias Without Moonlight

The American South from Regional
Confederacy to National Integration

Sheldon Hackney

Transaction Publishers
New Brunswick (U.S.A.) and London (U.K.)

Library of Congress Catalog Number: 2005050639
ISBN: 0-7658-0293-7
Printed in the United States of America

Library of Congress Cataloging-in-Publication Data

Hackney, Sheldon, 1933-
    Magnolias without moonlight : the American South from regional confederacy to national integration / Sheldon Hackney.
        p. cm.
    Includes bibliographical references.
    ISBN 0-7658-0293-7 (alk. paper)
    1. Southern States—Social conditions. 2. Social psychology—Southern States. 3. Southern States—History—20th century. 4. Southern States—Politics and government—1865-   I. Title.

HN79.A13H33   2005
306'.0975'0904—dc22   2005050639

Contents

Introduction

The title of this book is a parody of the cliché, "Moonlight and Magnolias," that itself is a mocking reference to a fanciful view of the ante-bellum South as a land of happy slaves, gracious plantation mistresses, kind masters, exquisite mansions, a code of honor, and a brave commitment to a non-commercial society based upon humane values. That invented South was the product of the need of white Southerners to justify slavery before the Civil War, and to salve the pain of defeat after the war. It also did remarkable service as cultural camouflage for economic self-interest on the part of leaders of the New South during and following Reconstruction. Then, in the nation's capitalist drive toward industrialization and urbanization in the late nineteenth and early twentieth centuries, creative Yankees manufactured nostalgia and sold it to a public in need of psychological relief from the stress of rapid change. This "Song of the South," to use the title of the Disney film version, has not deterred scholars from providing more realistic analyses, especially in the period following World War II. I wish to distinguish the essays in this volume from the romantic myth and to claim legitimacy in the scholarly tradition.

In another sense, however, this book can be understood as an expression of a different southern mythic tradition, the dream of Southern liberals to achieve racial and social justice, abolish poverty, and eliminate ignorance in the South without sacrificing those aspects of Southern culture that are admirable: the high value placed upon personal relationships; the recognition that manners are a signal that one accepts one's moral obligations to others, obligations that make civilized society possible; the importance of honor; the centrality of family; a sense of place; the awareness of how the past impinges on the present; respect for the community of others; and similar traditional values. In this light, these essays are part of my conversation with the Agrarians and C. Vann Woodward.

I began studying the American South years ago as an undergraduate at Vanderbilt University, a place saturated in the aura of the Agrarians, the remarkable group of intellectuals that included a rich concentration of modernist literary giants. Curiously, they criticized modernity in their 1930 manifesto, *I'll Take My Stand*.[1] They were decrying the coarsening of life that is the inevitable effect of rising standards of living made possible by industrialization. Their golden age was in the past but it was not the "cavaliers" who were their heroes. Their ideal citizens were the "plain folks" about whom one of their number, Frank L. Owsley, wrote. It is safe to assume that those plain folks were rushing to towns and cities within and without the South to embrace dehumanizing industrialism and the creature comforts it promised. With regard to the Agrarians, I was in awe but not in thrall.

After time out for service in the Navy, I went to Yale to continue my studies under the tutelage of C. Vann Woodward, a historian with moral and political commitments much more like my own. He was also the scholar who was reshaping the field of Southern history and playing a huge role in American intellectual life in general. My debt to him, as well as the country's debt, should be evident in two pieces included in this collection, "*Origins of the New South* in Retrospect, Thirty Years Later," and "C. Vann Woodward, In Memoriam."

I realize now that my original interest in the history of the South stemmed from my desire to understand myself better. Life, in part, is a voyage of self-discovery. Little secrets about ourselves are revealed as byproducts of action, of doing things, or of trying and failing. As we become more and more self-aware, we become increasingly free, more able to choose the person we want to be, limited only by the opportunities our society provides and by our personal inclinations, inclinations that are shaped by our culture. The existential dilemma is that we are both products of our culture and also authors of that culture. We are constantly negotiating between the self and its context. The more we know about the cultural streams in which we swim, the richer is our understanding of ourselves, and the more able we are to direct the course of our lives. These and other subtleties of the concept that is at the center of our national identity are traced in "Shades of Freedom."

I began my life of political awareness as a young, white, Protestant Southerner with an oppositional stance toward racial segregation, the existing orthodoxy in my hometown of Birmingham, Alabama. As I have written before, "For reasons that I find difficult to explain, but that probably have to do with my religious training, I had broken away from Southern white orthodoxy even before going to college and had concluded that racial segregation was wrong."[2] My relationship to my native region was therefore ambivalent. In several of the essays that follow you will find me arguing that even in its complexity and unceasing change, the Southern identity is rooted in biracialism. Every Southerner, black and white, must locate himself somehow in relationship to the successive biracial regimes in the South. My choice in that regard was early and evident. These essays reflect my choice as they explore aspects of the Southern identity and how they have changed over time.

There are at least two reasons for a non-Southerner to be interested in Southern history, other than the simple fact that the history of any society can add to our understanding of the human experience and the human condition. First, the South exists in opposition to the American non-south. The myth of the South was created by white Southerners trying to convince themselves that they were better than the abolitionists, their tormentors from outside the region. The myth was also used, however, by non-Southerners as a way of criticizing American civilization, and as psychic compensation for the brutal and crass realities of the modernizing North. So, the cultural construction of the South is a mirror image of the American identity. If you want to understand yourself as an American, one approach would be to learn to understand some "other" American. The South is both American and an exception to American at the same time. I explore these themes in "The South as a Counterculture," and "The Contradictory South."

Second, in two eras of American history, the South was the site of the central domestic political conflict: during the period leading up to and including the Civil War and Reconstruction, and then from the *Brown* decision in 1954 through the assassination of Martin Luther King, Jr. in 1968, when the civil rights movement was ignited in the South and then spread geographically to the rest of the country and demographically to other oppressed groups. All of the social justice movements that are still grist for our twenty-first century political mill originated in the sixties, inspired by the civil rights movement and the antiwar movement.

The realignment of American politics that came as a result of the Voting Rights Act of 1965, and as a reaction against the social justice and counter-cultural movements of the 1960s, still defines the American political scene. A disproportional number of the leaders of both parties now speak with southern accents. In the presidential election of 2004, the South was the most Republican region of the country. I subject these phenomena to intense, if ironic, analysis in "Identity Politics, Southern Style."

The character of society in the southern colonies was fixed rather early when economically ambitious Europeans entered the country, desiring to accumulate wealth in land so as to emulate the English landed aristocracy. They found fertile low land in a countryside penetrated by navigable rivers, suitable for staple crops (tobacco, wheat, rice, cotton) that could be sold in distant markets. The availability of cheap and malleable labor, a euphemism for slavery, fixed the character of settlement so that the population was dispersed across the countryside, with relatively few cities and towns. This yielded a simple social structure with a scarcity of nooks and crannies in which dissident voices could be nourished and sustained. It was therefore possible, when the nineteenth-century abolitionist movement gathered momentum, for the South to create itself as a closed society, inhospitable to either ideas or people that might threaten the status quo.

The Civil War, with its mixture of death, destruction and promised freedom, reinforced the notion of the South as an exception to the national narrative. The defeat of the Confederate States of America ended the grotesque institution of slavery and plunged the ex-CSA states into economic ruin. There was for a time the possibility that the freedmen, newly made citizens and enfranchised, would have a chance to achieve equality. It was not to be. The white South was able to defeat the First Reconstruction by using fraud, intimidation, and violence against freedmen and white dissidents at the local level, while waiting for the North to lose interest in the plight of black Americans in the South. National reconciliation was thus accomplished at the expense of black rights. Those rights were abrogated between 1890 and 1910 by legally codified racial segregation and disfranchisement. The South was allowed by the nation and by its own leaders to sink into a condition represented in the image of the Benighted South.

Despite some brave efforts at humane reform and economic progress, the region remained poor and underdeveloped until outside forces, unleashed by mobilization for World War II, hurried the belated industrialization and urbanization of the South. The Second Reconstruction that we call the civil rights movement therefore occurred in a region substantially different from the South of the late nineteenth century, and also in a nation more receptive to the possibilities of full citizenship for black Americans. The Second Reconstruction was successful in dismantling the legal structures of racial segregation and disfranchisement, but the unintended consequence was a political reorientation of the nation, ushering in a conservative hegemony under which the nation still lives.

As Rayford Logan termed it, the "nadir" of race relations was the period during which the Jim Crow system was put into law, and when blacks were forced out of electoral politics in the solidly Democratic South. Paradoxically, the modern struggle for equal rights began at that same low point. One might point to the founding of the NAACP in 1909 as the emblematic moment. From that point onward, there was an organized movement in the black community, assisted at times by white allies, to achieve equal rights for African Americans.

The mass-movement phase of the freedom struggle, beginning with perhaps the Montgomery bus boycott of 1955-56, was the result of the push of the black freedom struggle aided by the pull of a more receptive white public opinion. During the first half of the twentieth century, scholarly opinion made scientific racism a fringe ideology that could not be sustained in polite company. Black service in World War II meant thousands of returning servicemen who wanted at home something like the freedom for which they had been fighting overseas. The onset of the Cold War provided a geopolitical reason for the federal government to defend equal rights for nonwhite Americans. Furthermore, as Harry Truman demonstrated in 1948, there were strategically powerful black communities in the North, the result of the Great Migration of World War I and World War II. In the South, the prosperity stimulated by the industrialization of World War II, and the integration of the southern economy into the nation's, produced black communities in the South capable of organizing and sustaining mass protests. Most important, the advent of television made it possible for the nation to observe the dramas of injustice the movement staged in the South, as I point out in "The Little Rock Crisis and the American Dream."

The cycle of change repeatedly initiated by the modern civil rights movement would begin with racial confrontation in the South, then spread by way of sympathetic response in the North stimulated by print journalism and television coverage, producing a public opinion that allowed intervention in some form by the federal government, including especially the passage of the Civil Rights Act of 1964 and the Voting Rights Act of 1965.

In my telling here, the mass movement phase of the black freedom struggle was made possible by economic modernization. This is the reverse of what southern white liberals in the first half of the twentieth century thought. Their belief was that economic progress in the South would be possible only when there was some semblance of racial justice. Racial oppression and the backward economy were mutually reinforcing, which is why change in the South before the civil rights movement of the 1950s and 1960s depended upon the intervention of outside forces. That is also why political dissidence in the South has been fraught with difficulty, from populism in the 1890s to today, as the reader will detect from my essay, "The Clay County Origins of Mr. Justice Black."

That things in the South have changed, and changed for the better, is abundantly clear. Nevertheless, regional personality persists. A tendency toward the use of physical force to resolve disputes is a trait that I examined in 1969 in "Southern Violence." In that essay I confirm the popular perception of the South as unusually violent, and I demonstrate that it is more violent than would be predicted by the usual characteristics that one associates with murder, such as poverty, urbanization, and ignorance. There is something "Southern" about homicide.

Southern fascination with force still exists. In 2003, there were only eleven states in the union that executed prisoners; seven of those were ex-Confederate states. The death penalty was carried out in sixty-four cases by states; forty-three of those were in the South. Texas, the home of our president, is the champion of the death penalty in 2003 with twenty-four executions.

Violence in various forms, especially racially motivated mob violence, contributes to one of the images of the South, the cartoon of it as backward and benighted. That image gives rise to the white South's defensive mentality.

When Neil Young chastised the South in song, Lynyrd Skynyrd was honor-bound to reply. Young sang in "Southern Man:"

> Southern Man better keep your head
> Don't forget what your good book said
> Southern change gonna come at last
> Now your crosses are burning fast
> Southern man

In traditional self-defense mode, Lynyrd Skynrd responded in "Sweet Home Alabama":

> Well, I heard Mister Young sing about her.
> Well, I heard ole Neil put her down.
> Well, I hope Neil Young will remember
> A southern man don't need him around anyhow.
>> Sweet home Alabama where the skies are so blue.
>> Sweet home Alabama, Lord, I'm coming home to you.

Notes

1. John Crow Ransom, Allen Tate, Donald Davidson, Robert Penn Warren, Frank L. Owsley, Lyle Lanier, Herman Clarence Nixon, John Donald Wade, Stark Young, Andrew Lytle, Henry Blue Kline, and John Gould Fletcher.
2. Sheldon Hackney, The Politics of Presidential Appointment: A Memoir of the Culture War (Montgomery: New South Books, 2002), p. 145.

1

Southern Violence

A tendency toward violence has been one of the character traits most frequently attributed to Southerners.[1] In various guises, the image of the violent South confronts the historian at every turn: dueling gentlemen and masters whipping slaves, flatboatmen indulging in rough-and-tumble fights, lynching mobs, country folk at a bearbaiting or a gander pulling, romantic adventures of Caribbean filibusters, brutal police, panic-stricken communities harshly suppressing real and imagined slave revolts, robed night riders engaged in systematic terrorism, unknown assassins, church burners, and other less physical expressions of a South whose mode of action is frequently extreme.[2] The image is so pervasive that it compels the attention of anyone interested in understanding the South.

H. C. Brearly was among the first to assemble the quantitative data to support the description of the South as "that part of the United States lying below the Smith and Wesson line."[3] He pointed out, for example, that during the five years from 1920 to 1924 the rate of homicide per 100,000 population for the Southern states was a little more than two and a half times greater than for the reminder of the country. Using data from the *Uniform Crime Reports* concerning the 1930's, Stuart Lottier confirmed and elaborated Brearley's findings in 1938. For this period also he found that homicide was concentrated in the southeastern states. Of the eleven former Confederate states, Louisiana showed the lowest homicide rate, but it was 74 percent greater than the national average, and no non-Southern state had a higher rate. It is interesting that while murder and assault were oriented to the southeastern states, robbery rates were highest in the central and western states.[4] These findings were replicated in 1954 using data on crime for the years 1946-1952.[5] The pattern of high rates of serious crimes against persons and relatively lower rates of crimes against property for the South is consequently quite stable.

This essay first appeared in the *American Historical Review* LXXIV, No. 3 February 1969), 906-925. The copyright is held by the American Historical Association.

At the time that Bearley was setting forth the evidence for Southern leadership in physical aggression against people, another statistical study primarily of American suicide rates revealed that the
South was the area in which people had the least propensity to
destroy themselves.[6] Austin Porterfield, in 1949, using mortality
tables from *Vital Statistics of the United States*, brought the murder and the suicide indexes together and showed that there was a
general inverse relationship between the two rates among the states
and that the South ranked highest in homicide and lowest in suicide.[7] In 1940 the national average rate of suicide per 100,000
population was 14.4 and of homicide was 6.2, but the old and
cosmopolitan city of New Orleans had a suicide rate of 11.1 and a
homicide rate of 15.5. Even though some Southern cities exceed
some non-Southern cities in suicide rates, the New Orleans pattern of more homicides than suicides is typical of the South but
not of the nation. Porterfield comments that "suicide in every non-
Southern city exceeds homicide by ratios ranging from 1.19 to
18.60, while suicide rates exceed homicide rates in only eight of
the forty-three Southern and Southwestern cities, five of these being in the Southwest."[8]

Violence in the South has three dimensions. In relation to the
North, there are high rates of homicide and assault, moderate rates
of crime against property, and low rates of suicide. The relationship
between homicide and suicide rates in a given group is best expressed by a suicide-homicide ratio (SHR=100 [Suicides/
Suicides+Homicides]). The European pattern, shared by white Northerners but not by blacks or white Southerners, is for suicides to far
outnumber homicides so that the SHR is in excess of 80. The ratios
in table 1.1, displayed graphically in figure 1.1, Measure the difference between Southerners and other Americans with regard to violence. Because the statistics for "the United States" include the statistics for the Southern states, the differences between Southern and
non-Southern suicide-murder ratios are understated. Even so, the
differences are significant. In the North and the South, but more so
in the South, blacks commit murder much more often than they
commit suicide. Among white Americans, Southerners show a relatively greater preference than do non-Southerners for murder rather
than suicide.

Table 1.1
Suicide-Homicide Ratios for Four Categories of Americans, 1920-1964[9]

Year	United States White SHR	Southern White SHR	United States Negro SHR	Southern Negro SHR
1920	69.3	43.4*	11.2	05.6*
1925	70.9	53.5*	9.2	05.0*
1930	75.0	61.1*	11.9	06.0*
1935	96.2	59.9	11.4	6.3
1940	83.3	68.5	9.6	6.5
1945	80.3	66.4	11.1	6.8
1950	82.4	69.8	12.4	9.3
1955	88.3	73.1	15.6	9.7
1960	82.0	74.4	17.0	12.2
1964	81.1	73.2	16.7	11.1

Figure 1.1

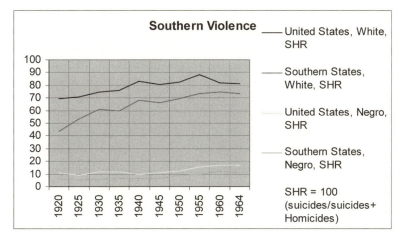

High murder and low suicide rates constitute a distinctly Southern pattern of violence, one that must rank with the caste system and
ahead of mint juleps in importance as a key to the meaning of being
Southern. Why this should be so is a question that has puzzled investigators for a long time, and their answers have been various.
When one loyal Southerner was asked by a probing Yankee why the
murder rate in the South was so high, he replied that he reckoned
there were just more folks in the South who needed killing.

Few apologies surpass this one in purity, but there is a more popular one that tries to explain the high homicide rates in the Southern states by the extremely high rates of violence among blacks, who constitute a large part of the population. As table 1.1 indicates, however, Southern whites considered by themselves vary from the national norm in the same direction as blacks, though to a much lesser extent. In addition, Porterfield points out that for the twelve Southern states with the heaviest black population, the coefficient of correlation between serious crimes and the percentage of blacks in the population is -.44. There is actually a tendency for states to rank lower in serious crimes as the percentage of blacks in the population increases.[10]

A more sophisticated theory is that Southern white society contains a larger proportion of lower status occupations so that the same factors that cause lower status groups in the North to become more violent than the rest of society have a proportionately greater effect on the South. The difference in rates would then be accounted for by the numerical bulge in the high-risk group, and only the stratification of society would be peculiarly Southern. Unfortunately for this theory, Southern cities, in which whites show the distinctive pattern of Southern violence, actually have greater percentages of the white population in higher status jobs than do Northern cities.[11] It is not the class structure that causes the Southern skew in the statistics.

In the same way, the agricultural nature of Southern life might account for the pattern of Southern violence. That the peculiar configuration exists in Southern cities swell as in the countryside could possibly be accounted for by the large migration into the city of people who learned their ways of living and dying in the country. Table 1.2 shows that both homicide and suicide rates are lower for rural districts than for urban areas. This results in a SHR for the white population of rural districts considered by themselves of 80.1, as compared with a SHR of 83.7 for the white population of the nation as a whole. The SHR of 68.8 in 1940 for Southern whites, both urban and rural, is significantly lower than the national ratio and indicates that Southern whites tended more to act out their aggressions than the white population of either the cities or the countryside in the rest of the nation.

Another way of testing the notion that the rurality of the South may be the root of its strange configuration of violence is summarized in table 1.3, a comparison of the SHR's of the eleven former Confederate states with those of the eleven most rural non-Southern

Table 1.2
Homicide and Suicide Rates by Race and by Size of Population Group,
United States, 1940[12]

	US	Cities 100,000 and up	Cities 10,000 - 100,000	Cities 2,500 - 10,000	Rural
Suicide					
(All Ages, Both Sexes					
All Races	14.4	16.8	15.6	15.1	12.0
White	15.5	17.8	16.4	16.0	13.3
Nonwhite	4.6	7.2	5.8	4.5	3.0
Homicide					
(All Ages, Both Sexes)					
All Races	6.2	7.1	5.7	7.3	5.7
White	3.1	3.2	2.5	3.7	3.3
Nonwhite	33.3	43.3	43.0	51.9	23.1

states. The non-Southern states, mostly Western, are closer in time to frontier days and are currently much more subject to instability caused by in-migration than are the Southern states, but otherwise the two sets of states are similar enough for purposes of comparison. In 1940, the percentage of population living in the urban areas of the Southern states ranged from 13.4 percent to 36.7 percent, with the mean falling at 26.1 percent, while in the eleven non-Southern states the degree of urbanization ranged from 13.6 percent to 36.7 percent, with the mean at 31.2 percent. In order not to distort the picture more than necessary, Nevada, with an extraordinary suicide rate of 41.3 per 100,000 population, is omitted from the comparison. At the same time, Virginia and Florida, with non-Southern SHR's, are retained in the Southern sample. The results still show a significant difference between the suicide-murder ratio of the Southern states and that of the most rural non-Southern states. The strange bent of Southern violence cannot be accounted for by the rural nature of Southern society.

Poverty is also a logical factor to suspect as the underlying cause of the South's pattern of violence. Howard Odum computed that in 1930 the Southeast had 20.9 percent of the nation's population but only 11.9 percent of its wealth.[14] Whether or not the region was poor before it was violent is undetermined. Even more to the point, poverty alone cannot explain high homicide rates. The decline of homicides during business depressions in the United States underlies this argument, as does the fact that crimes among second-generation immigrants are much higher than among first-generation immigrants despite increased material welfare of the former.[15] One study has found no significant correlation between crime rates and the propor-

Table 1.3
Suicide and Homicide Rates and Suicide-Homicide Ratios for Southern States and Eleven Most Rural Non-Southern States, 1940[13]

Population Group	Suicide-Homicide Ratio
Southern Nonwhite	6.7
National Nonwhite	12.2
Southern White	68.8
Nonsouthern, White Rural (11 states)	79.0
National White Rural	80.1
National White	83.7

Southern States	White		Rural Nonsouthern States	White	
	Suicide Rate	Homicide Rate		Suicide Rate	Homicide Rate
Alabama	11.7	6.9	Arizona	15.2	7.5
Arkansas	8.0	5.1	Idaho	17.7	3.3
Florida	19.8	7.5	Iowa	15.2	1.3
Georgia	12.1	5.6	Kansas	13.0	1.1
Louisiana	12.4	5.5	Montana	21.1	4.8
Mississippi	10.1	5.7	Nebraska	16.8	.7
North Carolina	10.4	4.0	New Mexico	14.2	5.7
South Carolina	9.7	5.0	North Dakota	9.7	1.4
Tennessee	10.0	7.1	South Dakota	10.5	1.8
Texas	13.6	5.3	Vermont	16.7	.8
Virginia	18.4	5.0	Wyoming	23.5	4.5
Average	12.4	5.6	Average	15.8	4.2

tion of the population on relief by county in Minnesota, whereas there was a strong correlation between crime rates and the degree of urbanization. Like the rural poor in Minnesota, the Japanese of Seattle were poor but honest and nonviolent.[16]

Though the data are extremely questionable, there is, nevertheless, a significant positive correlation between the SHR for the fifty-six world polities for which information is readily available and almost every measure of modernization that can be quantified.[17] It is difficult to determine whether it is underdevelopment or the process of change that accounts for this, for scholars have noted that the process of modernization generates various sorts of conflict and violence.[18] For both developing and industrialized nations, education is the most powerful predictor of a country's SHR, but indexes of industrial and urban activity, along with reflections of the society's general welfare, are also significantly correlated with the SHR. This is true for the fifty-six world polities considered together as well as for the European nations as a group and for the non-European countries taken together. That Southerners over the past half-century have been growing more similar to non-Southern Americans in their tastes in violence as the gap between the nation and the South in economic development has slowly narrowed also argues that there may be no increment of violence in the South that is not "explained" by the relative slowness of the region's development.

Multiple regression analysis offers a technique for testing the possibility that variations in the key indexes of modernization operating in an additive fashion might account for the South's particularity in rates of violence. Six independent variables measuring the four factors of wealth, education, urbanization, and age are included in this analysis. Except where indicated below, their values are taken from the *United States Census* for 1940. Urbanization is stated as the percentage of the population living within towns of 2,500 or more; education is measured by the median number of school years completed by persons twenty-five years old and older; "income" is the state's per capita personal income in dollars for 1940; unemployment is expressed as the percentage of the working force out of work; "wealth" is the state's per capita income in dollars in 1950; and age is the median age of the population. The values of each variable except "income" are recorded by race. "South" is a dummy variable included in the analysis in order to see if any of the unexplained residue of the dependent variable is associated with the fact of its occurring either inside our outside the South. All of the former Confederate states were assigned the value of one, while all non-Southern states were recorded as zero. The dependent variables that require "explaining" are the suicide rate, the homicide rate, the sum of the suicide rate and homicide rate, and the suicide-homicide ratio. Even though these rates are taken from the most reliable source, *Vital Statistics of the United States*, there may be large errors between the published rates and the true rates. Some violent deaths are never recorded, and many are improperly classified, but there is no reason to suspect that there has been a long-term, systematic bias in the collection and recording of the statistics for the Southern states. For the purpose of the crude comparison between South and non-South, the *Vital Statistics* are acceptable.

The results of the analysis are summarized in table 1.4. The coefficient of correlation between each of the independent variables and the dependent variable is found in the column labeled "Simple." The percentage of the variation in the dependent variable that is associated with, and thus "explained" by, the variation in the independent variable is found by squaring the coefficient of correlation. Education, for example, is the best single predictor of the white suicide rate. The simple coefficient of correlation of .62 between education and suicide in table 1.4 indicates that approximately 30 percent of the variation in the white suicide rate among the forty-eight states in 1940 is associated with variations in the educational level of the populations. The positive correlation means that the suicide rate tends to rise from one state to the next as the educational level rises. The negative coefficients of correlation between each of the independent variables, except South, and the white homicide rate indicate, conversely, that the homicide rate tends to decline as the indexes of development rise.

The effect on the dependent variable of all of the independent variables considered together is measured by the coefficient of multiple correlation, "R." Thus 72 percent of the white suicide rate and 52 percent of the white homicide rate are explained by the seven independent variables operating in an additive fashion. The coefficient of partial correlation expresses the relationship of each independent variable with the unexplained portion of the dependent variable after the independent variables acting collectively have done all the explaining possible. The coefficient of partial correlation for the dummy variable (South) is the most important yield of the multiple regression analysis.

Even though the seven independent variables acting together explain 72 percent of the variation of the white SHR among the forty-eight states in 1940, 28 percent (r= - .53) of the remaining portion of the variation of the white SHR is associated with the South. This means that the white SHR is lower in the South than can be accounted for by the lower indexes of urbanization, education, wealth, and age. There is, similarly, a significant portion of the variation from state to state in the white homicide rate, and in the white suicide rate, that is not explained by variations in measures of development, but that is explained by Southerness.

If the deviation of the South from the national norms for violence cannot be attribute to backwardness, or at least not to the static measures of underdevelopment, there are other possible explanations that should be considered. The concept of anomie, developed by Emile Durkheim in his study, *Suicide*, in 1895, is frequently mentioned as an explanation of both homicide and suicide, Amonie has

Table 1.4
Multiple Regression Analysis
Violence, Development, and Sectionalism in the United States[19]

Dependent Variables by State	R2 Variation Explained	Urbanization		Education		Income		Unemployment		Wealth		Age		South	
		Simple	Partial	Simple	Partial	Simple	Partial	Simple	Partial	Simple	Partial	Simple	Partial	Simple	Partial
White Suicide Rate	.72*	.25	-.64*	.62*	.52	.56*	.14	.22	.33	.53*	.35	.55*	.59*	-.31	.42*
White Homicide Rate	.52*	-.45*	-.24	.09	-.42	-.42	.23	-.13	.26	-.42	-.12	-.58*	.24	.52*	.49*
White Homicide plus Suicide Rate	.57*	.07	-.59*	.44*	.36	.36	.20	.15	.35	-.34	.22	-.30	.41*	-.09	.50*
White Suicide-Homicide Ratio	.72*	.53*	-.02	.11	.63*	.63*	-.24	.25	-.18	.62*	.29	.76*	.49*	-.68*	-.53*
Nonwhite Suicide Rate	0.30	.08	-.13	.25	.47*	.47*	.26	.15	-.09	.34	-.00	.13	-.04	-.34	.08
Nonwhite Homicide Rate	0.25	-.07	-.28	-.25	-.11	-.11	.18	-.17	.21	-.09	-.04	.04	.40*	.28	.37*
Nonwhite Homicide plus Suicide Rate	0.22	-.02	-.30	-.12	.13	.13	.27	-.08	.15	.09	-.04	.10	.35	.09	.37*
Nonwhite Suicide-Homicide Ratio	0.35	.27	.32	.31	.43*	.43*	.18	.30	-.11	.36	-.10	.12	-.40	-.36	-.09

meant slightly varying but not contradictory things to different investigators. It is most generally understood to be a social condition in which there is deterioration of belief in the existing set of rules of behavior, or in which accepted rules are mutually contradictory, or when prescribed goals are not accessible through legitimate means, or when cognition and socialization have been obstructed by personality traits that cluster about low ego-strength.[20] As it is manifested in the individual, in the form of anomy, it is a feeling of normlessness and estrangement from other people. An anomic person feels lost, drifting without clearly defined rules and expectations, isolated, powerless, and frustrated. In this state, there is a strong strain toward deviant behavior in various forms. The problem is that both homicide and suicide are thought to be related to it, and the theory does not predict what sorts of people or what groups will favor one form of behavior rather than another.

To look at Southern violence as the product of anomie in any case would involve a great paradox. The most popular explanation of the high rates of violence in America as compared to Europe places the blame on the rapid urbanization, secularization, and industrialization of the United States and on the social characteristics associated with this remarkable growth: Geographic and status mobility, an emphasis upon contractual relationships and striving, and a cultural pluralism that involves a high level of dissonance among the values that everyone tries to put into practice.[21] The South has traditionally served as the counterpoint to the American way of life because it seemed to differ from the North in these very aspects.[22] Southerners have a greater sense of history than Northerners, a greater attachment to place, and more deferential social customs. By all reports, Southerners place more emphasis on personal relations and on ascribed statuses than do Northerners. Not only do Southerners prize political and social cohesion, but by most measures the South is much more homogeneous than the non-South.[23] Yet, though the South differs from the North on so many of the factors that supposedly contribute to anomie and thus to violence, the South is the nation's most violent region.

One body of theory seems to predict higher rates of violence precisely because of the South's homogeneity. Reformulating the observations of George Simmel and Bronislaw Malinowski, Lewis Coser writes that "we may say that a conflict is more passionate and more radical when it arises out of close relationships." "The closer the relationship," so the reasoning goes, "the greater the affective investment, the greater also the tendency to suppress rather than express hostile feeling.... In such cases feelings of hostility tend to accumulate and hence intensify." Such a theory fits the empirical observation that individuals who express hostility retain fewer and less violent feelings of antagonism toward the source of their irritation.[24] But Coser himself states that, though conflicts within close relationships are likely to be intense when they occur, "this does not necessarily point to the likelihood of more frequent conflict in closer relationships than in less close ones." There are situations in which accumulated hostilities do not eventuate in conflict and may even serve to solidify the relationship.[25]

The frustration-aggression hypothesis involves similar perplexities.[26] One of the alternative ways of adapting to frustration is, for example, to turn the frustration inward upon the self. In extreme cases this can result in suicide.[27] A psychoanalyst has concluded after an extensive study that a major portion of Sweden's high suicide rate is caused by the frustrations arising from a highly competitive, success-oriented society.[28] The general rise in suicide rates in the United States during economic downturns argues that the same mechanism is at work among some segments of the population. Consequently, nothing in the frustration-aggression hypothesis predicts the direction the aggression will take.

There are currently two theories that attempt to explain the generally inverse relationship between homicide and suicide as reactions to frustration. The first, developed by Andrew F. Henry and James F. Short, Jr.,[29] is based on the assumption that both homicide and suicide are the result of frustration-aggression and builds upon Porterfield's initial suggestion that the strength of the relational system might have something to do with an individual's choice of either homicide or suicide.[30] Henry and Short adduce data on the relationship of homicide and suicide rates to the business cycle and to certain statistically distinct groups. They reason that overt aggression against others "varies directly with the strength of external restraint over the behavior of the adult-external restraint which is a function of strength of the relational system and position in the status hierarchy."[31] According to this theory, overt aggression increases as the strength of the relational system increases and as a person's position in the status hierarchy decreases.

Martin Gold has pointed out, however, that contrary to the hypothesis of Henry and Short, upper status people are likely to be more restrained by the expectations of others than are lower status people. Even more damaging is Gold's demonstration that the Henry and Short hypothesis does not correctly predict the greater preference of women for suicide rather than homicide;[32] nor does it correctly predict that suicide rates are lower among the middle classes than at either extreme of the social scale.

The second theory, fashioned by Gold, attempts to relate differences in child-rearing practices to preferences for hostility or guilt as an accommodation to frustration. Gold shows specifically that there is a positive correlation between the incidence of physical punishment commonly used in the child-rearing practice of certain groups and the rate of homicide for that group. His conclusion is that physical disciplining of children leads to aggression against others rather than against the self.[33] To confound the theory, restrictive child-rearing practices in Europe evidently do not lead to the physical violence that such practices among the lower classes in America are supposed to produce. It is also doubtful that there is a significant class differential in the degree of physical punishment used to discipline children.[34] William and Joan McCord found in their study of juveniles that there was no strong relationship between disciplining methods and criminality except when a child is rejected by his parents or when his parents provide him with a deviant role model; harsh discipline does less damage than neglect.[35] Despite such complexities, it is reasonable to suppose that there is some causal relationship between the socialization of aggression and a group's SHR, but before such a relationship can be a useful ingredient of an explanation of Southern violence, anthropologists and historians need to know much more about regional differences in child-rearing techniques.

Whether or not the cause can be located in child-rearing practices, several bodies of evidence point to the conclusion that Southern violence is a cultural pattern that exists separate from current influences. For instance, several commentators have suggested that the habit of carrying guns in the South made murder a much more frequent outcome of altercations among Southerners than among Northerners. This argument is buttressed by a 1968 survey, reported in table 1.5, which showed that 52 percent of Southern white families owned guns, as opposed to 27 percent of their non-Southern white counterparts.

Table 1.5
Percent of Families Owning Firearms[36]

	Yes	No	Not Sure
Total White	34	65	1
South	52	45	3
Non-South	27	72	1
Total Non-White	24	70	6
South	34	61	5
Non-South	15	78	7

It may be, however, that this differential in ownership of guns is the result of a violent turn of mind rather than the cause of violence. This is the implication of the fact that when the House of Representatives in 1968 passed a weak gun control bill to restrict the mail-order sale of rifles, shotguns, and ammunition by the overwhelming vote of 304 to 118, representatives of the eleven former Confederate states nonetheless voted 73 to 19 against the bill.[37] It should be noted, too, that while some Southern states have relatively strict firearms laws, these laws do not dramatically affect their homicide rates.[38]Furthermore, the assault rate is extremely high in the South, indicating that Southerners react with physical hostility even without guns.

A glance at table 1.4 reveals that for blacks either the data are grossly skewed or there is little relationship between violence and the selected indexes of social welfare. The barest hint exists that, controlling for the selected factors, there is some explanatory value in sectionalism, a conclusion that has independent verification. Thomas F. Pettigrew and Rosalind Barclay Spier found that the major correlate of the black homicide rate in the North was the proportion of blacks in a given area who had been born and raised in the South and that this was in addition to the effect of migration itself. It had long been know that homicide was much less frequent among Northern than among Southern blacks; this finding suggests that violence in the South is a style of life that is handed down from father to son along with the old hunting rifle and the family Bible.[39]

The great contribution to the discussion of Southern violence made by Wilbur J. Cash in his book *The Mind of the South* was precisely that Southern violence is part of a style of life that can only be explained historically.[40] According to Cash's own poetic and impressionistic rendering, violence grew up on the Southern frontier as naturally as it grew up on any frontier. Violence was an integral part of the romantic, hedonistic, hell-of-a-fellow personality created by the absence of external restraint that is characteristic of a frontier. The cult of honor, with it insistence on the private settlement of disputes, was one manifestation of the radical individualism of the South, but there were other influences at work. The plantation, the most highly organized institution of the Southern frontier, reinforced the tendency toward violence that had been initiated by the absence of organization. This was so, Cash argues, for two reasons: whites on the plantation exercised unrestrained dominance over blacks; and whites were generally raised by blacks and consequently were deeply influenced by the romantic and hedonistic black personality. Cash does not explicitly say what forces produced this black personality, but the implication is that it is fixed by the laws of genetics. But if the more likely position is taken that black and white personalities are shaped by environment and experience, then the reader is left with yet another Cashian paradox: violence in the white personality stems at the same time from the effect of being unrestrained and from imitating the black personality which was formed out of a situation of dependency and subordination.

The mediating variable that brings together the various inconsistencies in Cash's explanation of how violence came to be established in the late antebellum period as part of the Southern personality may be the absence of law. Not disorganization, not individualism, not dominance nor submission, not lack of restraint-none of these forces played as important a role as the absence of institutions of law enforcement in compelling Southerners to resort to the private settlement of disputes. Cash makes it explicit in his treatment of Reconstruction, the second frontier.

During Reconstruction, according to Cash, Southern whites resorted to individual and collective violence because the courts were dominated by carpetbaggers and scalawags. Though this is logical it is not consistent with Cash's earlier argument that the growth of law had been inhibited on the antebellum frontier by the desire of Southerners to provide their own justice. Apparently the direction of causation in the relationship between law and violence changes in accordance with the needs of Cash's interpretation.

Just as the first and second Southern frontiers simultaneously promoted social solidarity and individualism, the third Southern frontier, progress, changed the South in the direction of the American norm of Babbittry while at the same time accommodating continuity in the basic traits of the Southern mind. A further paradox is involved in the impact of progress on the pattern of violence. Because violence originally arose from individualism, Cash says, the growth of towns should have brought a decrease in rates of violence. This decrease did not materialize because progress also brought poverty, and poverty destroys individualism. Cash argues in effect that individualism produced violence in the antebellum period and the loss of individualism produced violence in the twentieth century.

Though Cash failed to formulate a coherent theory of Southern violence, he did focus on two factors that are obvious possibilities as the chief motive forces of Southern violence: the frontier experience and the presence of blacks. The American frontier did spawn violence, but it seems improbable that the frontier could have much to do with the fact that in the twentieth-century Southern states on the eastern seaboard have much higher rates of violence than the nation at large. There is also considerable difficulty with the notion that the presence of large numbers of blacks account for the great propensity of whites for violence. There is, in fact, little interracial homicide,[41] and there is no reason to question John Dollard's hypothesis that Negroes murder and assault each other with such appalling frequency because of their daily frustrations in dealing with white men. Because aggression against whites would call forth extreme negative sanctions, frustrated blacks transfer their aggressive feeling to other blacks.[42] If this is the case, it is difficult to see how high rates of violence among the dominant white group would also be attributed to the white-black relationship, especially when the presence of blacks in the North is not accompanied by a proportionate rate of violence among the whites. It is also interesting that whites in South Africa who also experienced frontier conditions and a subordinate nonwhite population have a homicide-suicide ratio almost identical to the ratio of the American North but quite different from that of the South.

Subservience, rather than dominance, may be the condition that underlies a pattern of low SHR's. In his extremely popular book *The Wretched of the Earth*, Frantz Fanon suggests that the oppressed status of a colonial people produces a pattern of aggressiveness directed against fellow colonials and a need to achieve manhood through violence. The task of revolutionaries is to mobilize the aggressive drives, provide them a sustaining ideology, and direct them against the oppressors.[43] Defeat in the Civil War and the South's resulting position as an economic dependency of the industrial Northeast qualify it for consideration as a violent colonial region. In addition to the difficulty of separating the effects of subservience from the effects of sheer underdevelopment, the problem with this line of reasoning is that the heroic myths created about the Lost Cause and the relatively early return of home rule after the Civil War may have mitigated the trauma of defeat and social dislocation. It would be difficult to maintain that the South's historical experience as a region is the equivalent of the sort of cultural conflict that leads to the loss of self-esteem, disrupts the processes of socialization, and initiates the cycle of self-crippling behavior within the subordinate group. [44] Furthermore, American Indians have responded to their experience of defeat and repression with higher rates of suicide and other intrapunitive behavior rather than with aggression against others. Similarly, while industrialization was transforming and disrupting its established folk culture, Harlan County, Kentucky, had the highest homicide rate in the country, but a study of community growth in New England finds suicide and depressive disorders highly correlated with the disruptive impact of geographic mobility.[45] Though the social sciences offer no clearly authenticated hypothesis that predicts the relationship in different populations between homicide and suicide rates,[46] there are some potentially illuminating investigations currently in progress. Assuming that depressed mental patients are people who have turned anger inward through introjection and guilt when under chronic stress, while paranoid patients are those who have turned anger outward through denial and projection, one study has found an interesting association between the pattern of intrafamily communication and the direction taken by mental pathology when it occurred. Depressed patients in this study came from families in which as children they were forced to try by themselves to attain the desired forms of behavior through positive, "ought" channels. Paranoid patients came from families in which they were forced into acceptable modes of behavior by negative "ought not" procedures.

In families of *depressed* patients the child comes to view his environment as non-threatening to him physically. It is something to be manipulated by him in order to bring about the desired effects that will win approval. There is directionality here, and it is *from* the child *toward* his environment. On the other hand, in families of paranoid patients the child comes to view his environment as having potentially harmful properties that he cannot control and that must be avoided in some way. Here the directionality if *from* the environment *toward* the child.[47]

The hypothesis is that a manipulative attitude toward the environment will be associated with intrapunitive behavior and that a passive attitude toward the environment, with the absence of the internalization of a feeling of responsibility for the self, will be correlated with a greater use of projection in ego-defense.

There are firm indications that cultural patterning as well as childrearing techniques will affect the perception of the environment and the orientation of the personality on the paranoia-depression continuum. In Burma, a hierarchical society in which a person's prestige and authority increase as he gets older, the social and physical environment is typically perceived as potentially harmful, and Burma has one of the highest homicide rates in the world.[48] There is also the possibility of a connection between the high rates of violence among Afro-Americans and the recent diagnosis that the black psyche has been rendered paranoiac by the hostile American environment. [49]

Testing the hypothesis that a paranoid perception of the environment is the root cause of the pattern of violence in the white South is a problem for future scholarship. The most immediately useful technique would be a survey of attitudes toward violence, perceptions of the environment, feelings of personal efficacy, and other measures of alienation. There may be regional differentials in these categories as well as class, age, and sexual differentials. A rigorous comparison of rates of violence in perhaps a Kentucky county and an Ohio county at comparable stages of settlement is also a promising approach. The records of the county court, the reports of the state attorney general, and newspaper surveys might produce useful data on both individual and collective violence. Some effort must be made to determine when the South became violent; timing may reveal much about the relationship of slavery to violence. The possible effects of Scotch-Irish immigration, population density, temperature, and religious fundamentalism should be investigated with quantitative methods. Even though the SHR's of Australia and Canada fit the European mold, some insight may derive from pursuing such comparative cases in a detailed manner. Much can be done.

Meanwhile, in the search for a valid explanation of Southern violence the most fruitful avenue will probably be one that seeks to identify and trace the development of a Southern world view that defines the social, political, and physical environment as hostile and casts the white Southerner in the role of the passive victim of malevolent forces. When scholars locate the values that make up this worldview and the process by which it was created and is transmitted, the history of the South will undoubtedly prove to have played a major role. The un-American experiences of guilt, defeat, and poverty will be major constituents of the relevant version of that history,[50] but perhaps they will not loom so large as the sense of grievance that is at the heart of the Southern identity.

Southern self-consciousness was created by the need to protect a peculiar institution from threats originating outside the region. Consequently, the Southern identity has been linked from the first to a siege mentality. Though Southerners have many other identities, they are likely to be most conscious of being Southerners when they are defending their region against attack from outside forces: abolitionists, the Union Army, carpetbaggers, Wall Street and Pittsburgh, civil rights agitators, the federal government, feminism, socialism, trade-unionism, Darwinism, Communism, atheism, daylight-saving time, and other by-products of modernity. This has produced an extreme sensitivity to criticism from outsiders and a tendency to excuse local faults as the products of forces beyond human or local control. If the South was poor, it was because the Yankees stole all the family silver and devastated the region in other ways after the Civil War. If industrialization seemed inordinately slow in the South, it was because of a conspiracy of Northern capitalists to maintain the region as an economic colony. Added to this experience with perceived threats have been the fact that almost every significant change in the life of the South has been initiated by external powers. This is even true of industrialization. Though there was a fervent native movement to sponsor industrialization, absentee ownership has been characteristic. Furthermore, the real qualitative change in the Southern pattern of low-wage industry came as a result of World War II and the activities of the federal government.

Being Southern, then, inevitably involves a feeling of persecution at times and a sense of being a passive, insignificant object of alien or impersonal forces. Such a historical experience has fostered a worldview that supports the denial of responsibility and locates threats to the region outside the region and threats to the person outside the self. From the Southern past arise the symbiosis of profuse hospitality and intense hostility toward strangers and the paradox that the Southern heritage is at the same time one of grace and violence.

Notes

1.   See, e.g., Charles O. Lerche, Jr., *The Uncertain South: Its Changing Patterns of Politics in Foreign Policy* (Chicago: Quadrangle Books, 1964, 48-49). Representative comments can be found in John Richard Alden, *The South in the Revolution. 1763-1789* (Baton Rouge: Louisiana State University Press, 1957), 34-35, 41; Clement Eaton, *A History of the Old South*, second edition (New York: Macmillan, 1966), 260-395,404,407,415; John Hope Franklin, *The Militant South, 1800-1861* (Cambridge, MA: Harvard University Press, 1956); David Bertelson, *The Lazy South* (New York: Oxford University Press, 1967), 101-13, 241; H. V. Redfield, *Homicide, North and South: Being a Comparative View of Crime Against the Person in Several Parts of the United States* (Philadelphia: J. B. Lippincott, 1880).

2.   A stimulating essay on this theme is Frank Vandiver, "The Southerner as Extremist," in *The Idea of the South* (Chicago: University of Chicago Press, 1964), 43-56. A lighter treatment of the same subject is Erskine Caldwell, "The Deep South's Other Venerable Tradition," *New York Times Magazine*, July 11, 1965, 10-18.

3.   H. C. Brearley, "The Pattern of Violence," in *Culture in the South*, ed. W. T. Couch (Chapel Hill: University of North Carolina Press, 1934), 678-92; and H. C. Brearley, *Homicide in the United States* (Chapel Hill: University of North Carolina Press, 1932).

4.   Stuart Lottier, "Distribution of Criminal Offenses in Sectional Regions," *Journal of Criminal Law and Criminology,* XXIX (Sept.-Oct. 1938), 329-44.

5.   Lyne Shannon, "The Spatial Distribution of Criminal Offenses by States," *ibid.,* XLV (Sept.-Oct. 1954), 264-73.

6.   Louis I. Dublin and Bessie Bunzel, *To Be Or Not To Be: A Study of Suicide* (New York: Smith and Haas, 1933), 80, 413.

7.   Austin L. Porterfield, "Indices of Suicide and Homicide by States and Cities: Some Southern-Non-Southern Contrasts with Implications for Research," *American Sociological Review,* XIV (Aug. 1949, 481-90.

8.   Ibid., 485.

9.   Suicide-Homicide Ratio = 100 (Suicides/Suicides+Homicides). As the ratio approaches 100, it registers the increasing preference for suicide rather than murder among the members of a given group. The ratios were computed from figures taken from Forrest E. Linder and Robert D. Grove, *Vital Statistics Rates in the United States, 1900-1940* (Washington, D.C., 1943); and U.S., Department of Health, Education and Welfare, *Vital Statistics of the United States*, for the appropriate years. The asterisks in the table indicate that: in 1920 all of the former Confederate states were included in the figures except Alabama, Arkansas, Georgia, and Texas; Arkansas, Georgia, and Texas were still not reporting in 1925, but by 1930 only Texas was excluded; since 1935 all Southern states are included.

10.   Austin L. Porterfield, "A Decade of Serious Crimes in the United States," *American Sociological Review*, XIII (Feb. 1948), 44-54; see also James E. McKeown, "Poverty, Race, and Crime," *Journal of Criminal Law and Criminology*, XXXIX (Nov.-Dec. 1948), 480-83.

11.   Norvald Glenn, "Occupational Benefits to Whites from the Subordination of Negroes," *American Sociological Review,* XXVIII (June 1963), 443-48, esp. table 1.

12.   The source for this table is Linder and Grove, *Vital Statistics Rates in the United States, 1900-1940,* table 24.

13.   The source for Table III is *ibid.,* Table 20. All rates are per 100,000 population.

14.   Howard Odum, *Southern Regions of the United States* (Chapel Hill: University of North Carolina Press., 1936), 208.

15.   Edwin H. Sutherland and Donald R . Cressey, *Principles of Criminology,* 6th ed. (New York: J.B. Lippincott, 1960), 92, 146-69.

16.   Van B. Shaw, "The Relationship between Crime Rates and Certain Population Characteristics in Minnesota Counties," *Journal of Criminal Law and Criminology,* XL (May-June 1949), 43-49.

17.   Simple intercorrelations were run between the indexes of homicide and suicide and measures of social and economic activity using data from *World Handbook of Political and Social Indicators,* ed. Bruce M. Russett et al. (New Haven, CT: Yale University Press, 1964); and Statistical Office of the United Nations Department of Economic and Social Affairs, *Demographic Yearbook, 1963* (New York: United Nations Publications, 1964), table 25.

18.   Richard S. Weinert, "Violence in Pre-Modern Societies: Rural Colombia," *American Political Science Review,* LX (June 1966), 340-47; *Internal War, Problems and Approaches,* ed. Harry Eckstein (New York, 1964); E. J. Hobsbawm, *Primitive Rebels: Studies in Archaic Forms of Social Movement in the 19th and 20 th Centuries* (New York, 1959). An important synthesis and statement of theory is Ted Gurr, "Psychological Factors in Civil Violence," *World Politics,* XX (Jan. 1968), 245-78.

19.   The asterisks in the table denote that the chance that a random ordering of the data would produce a relationship this strong is less than one in one hundred.

20.   Herbert McClosky and John H. Scharr, "Psychological Dimension of Anomy," *American National Character* (Garden City, N.Y., 1963); C. Vann Woodward, *The Burden of Southern History* (Baton Rouge, La., 1960), 109-40.

21.   David Abrahamsen, *The Psychology of Crime* (New York, 1960), 18-21, 177-83. These relationships are greatly illuminated by the discussion in David Potter, *People of Plenty: Economic Abundance and the American Character* (Chicago, 1954).

22.   William H. Taylor, *Cavalier and Yankee: The Old South and American National Character* (Garden City, N.Y., 1963); C. Vann Woodward, *The Burden of Southern History* (Baton Rouge, La., 1960) 109-40.

23.   Jack P. Gibbs and Walter T. Martin, *Status Integration and Suicide: A Sociological Study* (Eugene, Ore., 1964), exp. table 6.

24.   Lewis A. Coser, *The Functions of Social Conflict* (New York, 1956), 57, 62, 71; Albert Pepitone and George Reichling, "Group Cohesiveness and Expression of Hostility," in *Personality and Social Systems,* ed, Neil J. Smelser and William T. Smelser (New York, 1963), 117-24.

25.   Coser, *Functions of Social Conflict,* 72.

26.   John Dollard et al*., Frustration and Aggression* (New Haven, Conn., 1939); Leonard Berkowitz, *Aggression: A Social Psychological Analysis* (New York, 1962); Aubrey J. Yates, *Frustration and Conflict* (New York, 1962).

27.   Karl Menninger, *The Man Against Himself* (New York, 1938), 23. The assumption that homicide and suicide are simply aggressions manifested in different directions is the basis of the concept of the suicide-homicide ratio.

28.   Herbert Hendin, *Suicide and Scandinavia: A Psychoanalytic Study of Culture and Character* (Garden City, N.Y., 1965) chap. V.

29.   Andrew F. Henry and James F. Short, Jr., *Suicide and Homicide: Some Economic, Sociological, and Psychological Aspects of Aggression* (Glencoe, Ill., 1954).

30.   Porterfield, "Indices of Suicide and Homicide," 488.

31.   Henry and Short, *Suicide and Homicide,* 119.

32.   Martin Gold, "Suicide, Homicide, and the Socialization of Aggression," *American Journal of Sociology,* LXIII (May 1958), 651-61. Gold originated the SHR, which he called the "suicide-murder ratio."

33. Ibid.
34. Melvin L. Kohn, "Social Class and the Exercise of Parental Authority," in *Personality and Social Systems,* ed. Smelser and Smelser, 297-314; Martha Sturm White, "Social Class, Child Rearing Practices, and Child Behavior," *ibid.*, 286-96; Bernard C. Rosen and Roy D'Andrade, "The Psychosocial Origins of Achievement Motivation," *Sociometry*, XXII (Sept. 1959), 185-215, cited in *Anomie and Deviant Behavior: A Discussion and Critique,* ed. Marshall B. Clinard (New York, 1964) 260-61; Bernard Berelson and Gary A. Steiner, *Human Behavior: An Inventory of Scientific Findings* (New York, 1964), 479-81.
35. William McCord and Joan McCord, *Origins of Crime: A New Evaluation of the Cambridge-Somerville Youth Study* (New York, 1959), 172, 198.
36. The source of Table V is a survey of national statistical sample by Opinion Research, Inc., for a Columbia Broadcasting System program, September 2, 1968.
37. *New York Times*, July 25, 1968.
38. Carl Bakal, *The Right to Bear Arms* (New York, 1966), 346-53.
39. Thomas F. Pettigrew and Rosalind Barclay Spier, "The Ecological Structure of Negro Homicide," *American Journal of Sociology*, LXVII (May 1962), 621-29.
40. Wilbur J. Cash, *The Mind of the South* (New York, 1940; Vintage ed., 1960), 32-34, 44-52, 76, 115-23, 161, 220, 424.
41. Marvin E. Wolfgang, *Patterns in Criminal Homicide* (Philadelphia, 1958), 222-36.
42. John Dollard, *Caste and Class in a Southern Town,* 3rd ed. (Garden City, N.Y., 1949), chap. XIII.
43. Franz Fanon, *The Wretched of the Earth* (New York, 1963).
44. Thomas Stone et al., "Poverty and the Individual," in *Poverty and Affluence*, ed. Leo Fishman (New Haven, Conn., 1966), 72-96.
45. Paul Frederick Cressey, "Social Disorganization and Reorganization in Harlan County, Kentucky," *American Sociological Review*, XIV (June 1949), 389-94; Henry Wechsler, "Community Growth, Depressive Disorders, and Suicide," *American Journal of Sociology,* LXVII (July 1961), 9-16.
46. Jack O. Douglas, *The Social Meanings of Suicide* (Princeton, N.J., 1967), 3-160.
47. Hazel M. Hitson and Daniel H. Funkenstein, "Family Patterns and Paranoidal Personality Structure in Boston and Burma" *International Journal of Social Psychiatry,* V (Winter, 1959).
48. Ibid.
49. William H. Grier and Price M. Cobbs, *Black Rage* (New York, 1968).
50. Woodward, *Burden of Southern History*, 3-26.

2

Origins of the New South in Retrospect

One of the facts of intellectual life that makes publishers happy and students sad is that every generation writes it own history. The elapse of more than the traditional span of two decades since the publication of *Origins of the New South* by C. Vann Woodward[1] makes it an appropriate time to wonder whether a new generation has begun to alter Woodward's masterful portrait of the South between 1877 and 1913. Of the three general sources of revisionist impulses—new information, new question, new world views—all have had ample time and sufficient cause to wash away Woodward's version of the origins of the New South. Yet, given the amazing frequency with which the generational waves are rolling over our cultural breakwaters, the remarkable thing is that there has been so little fundamental challenge to the outlines of the story established by Woodward twenty years ago.

Of one thing we may be certain at the outset. The durability of *Origins of the New South* is not a result of its ennobling and uplifting message. It is the story of the decay and decline of the aristocracy, the suffering and betrayal of the poor white, and the rise and transformation of a middle class. It is not a happy story. The Redeemers are revealed to be as venal as the carpetbaggers. The declining aristocracy are ineffectual and money hungry, and in the last analysis they subordinated the values of the political and social heritage in order to maintain control over the black population. The poor whites suffered from strange malignancies of racism and conspiracy-mindedness, and the rising middle class was timid and self-interested even in it reform movement. The most sympathetic characters in the whole sordid affair are simply those who are too powerless to be blamed for their actions.

Reprinted from *Journal of Southern History*, 38 (May 1972), 191-216.

Such a somber view differs sharply from the confident optimism exuded by the New South school of historians such as Philip Alexander Bruce, Broadus Mitchell, Paul H. Buck, and Holland Thompson.[2] Embellished by various degrees of hyperbole, their principal theme was that of sectional reconciliation and the casting off of the dead hand of the past. "Most of the real Southern colonels are dead," Holland Thompson wrote in 1919, "and the others are too busy running plantations or cotton mills to spend much time discussing genealogy, making pretty speeches, or talking about their honor. Not so many colonels are made as formerly, and one may travel far before he meets an individual who fits the popular idea of the type. He is likely to meet more men who are cold, hard, and astute, for the New South has developed some perfect specimens of the type whose natural habitat had been supposed to be Ulster or the British Midlands-religious, narrow, stubborn, and very shrewd."[3] "New South" for Thompson meant not only this new spirit of enterprise but a desire to accept the results of the Civil War as the best thing that could have happened, to face the future without rejecting the past, and the determination to play a part in national life. "Economically," Thompson maintained, "the South has prospered in proportion as the new spirit has ruled."[4]

Thompson himself was very cautious about his claims as regards the real economic changes in the South, but he was typical of the New South historians in many other things. In accord with the interpretation of Reconstruction then dominant that is associated with the name and work of William Archibald Dunning, Thompson viewed Reconstruction as a fiasco of disorder and dishonesty. Consequently, the men who returned the South to (conservative white) home rule, the Redeemers, appeared in a favorable light. Even though Thompson indulged in no cult of the Redeemers, he presented them as honest men justifiably concerned about white supremacy. Their only fault, according to Thompson, was perhaps an unhealthy fixation upon maintaining low taxes to the detriment of progressive services such as good schools and good roads. Toward the irrational and ill-informed rebellion of the Populists against their natural and traditional leaders, Thompson was condescendingly tolerant. Similarly, he pictured cotton-mill operatives as content with their lot except when stirred up by malcontents and agitators, and the political conflict of the Progressive movement is largely swallowed up in Thompson's account by the general swell of the developing social consciousness which resulted in humanitarian reforms and more schools, roads, and hospitals. The South looked to the future with a sense of well-being and optimism.

Though the Black Reconstruction myth already had been subjected to effective criticism by the time Woodward wrote, the buoyant picture of the succeeding era created by the New South historians still stood. It had been deflated neither by the attacks from the right by the Agrarians nor from the left by regionalists such as Howard W. Odum and Rupert B. Vance. Thus the themes that wound their way through *Origins of the New South*, camouflaged though they were by a gently seductive prose style and by subtle qualifications, were nonetheless a radical departure, one that not only veered to the left in response to Depression-era outlooks but that recast the story of the late nineteenth-century South. No longer could historians write as if the central conflict of the period pitted disembodied forces representing the agrarian past and the industrial future against each other. Henceforth the contending parties would be considerably more corporeal.

Phrased baldly, the thesis of *Origins of the New South* builds from the perception that though the Civil War deflected the course of southern history and altered the nature of southern society, there was considerable continuity between the policies of the Radical Republican governments of Reconstruction and the Conservative Democratic regimes established by the Redeemers. Regardless of who was in power, railroads and other special interests continued to enjoy privileges granted by government. The final act of Redemption itself took place as part of the electoral crisis of 1876-1877 when a Whiggish alliance between Southern Democrats and national Republicans arranged to swap the presidency for home rule, political patronage, and internal improvements, an arrangement made possible through the good offices of that selfless public servant, Thomas A. Scott of the Pennsylvania Railroad. Railroads were the only national force strong enough to bring the warring sections and parties together.

So, Redemption was not a restoration. The old planter aristocracy was not returned to power with the Democratic Party because the party had received a large admixture of Hamiltonian-Whig-industrial elements, dynamic components that quickly rose to the top of the party. Conservative in most matters, the *mesalliance* that was the Democratic Party was liberal in its use of fraud and violence to achieve Redemption, in its creation of a corrupt political system to maintain itself in power, and in the frequency with which its office-holders absconded with public funds. Frightening the poor whites into line with the specter of black domination and holding planter opposition within bounds by playing upon their fear of poor-white insurgency, the Redeemers captured the slogans of white supremacy and home rule and used these banners to cloak the pursuit of their own political and economic purposes. The history of the New South period, according to this view, is largely the story of how the Redeemers ruled in a manner that was against the interests of the mass of common people.

Debunking the Redeemers was one of the most important contributions of *Origins of the New South*. In their previous incarnation, they had been seen often as heroic statesmen and at worst as a trifle shortsighted because of their policies of minimum government and maximum financial stringency. Now it is clear that Redemption was no moral demarcation.

Nor was it an economic demarcation dividing a glorious agrarian past and a glorious industrial future, as the new South ideologues would have it. Despite their glowing rhetoric, the South had to run hard just to keep from losing ground. Over the period from 1877 to 1913 the South's percentage of the nation's manufacturing establishments and its share of capital engaged in manufacturing remained constant. Never, in fact, had the South been more distinct from the North in every measure of wealth and social well-being and never more similar in the values espoused by the leaders of the two sections. Contrary to what some previous historians had believed, according to the *Origins of the New South,* high profits as well as moral fervor account for the growth of cotton mills in the South, a growth that began long before the 1880 date emphasized by New South historians. Contrary also to the romantic notions of Wilbur J. Cash and Broadus Mitchell, members of the new middle class were not the sons of the old planter aristocracy. More often than not they derived from the families of urban merchants or men of the professions. Wherever they came from, economic history does not explain why the captains of industry were in control, because the industrial revolution simply did not happen.

The reasons for the slow rate of industrial development are not far to seek. The South's was a colonial economy. It remained overwhelmingly a region of staple-crop agriculture and extractive industries. This meant that southerners bought almost all their manufactured goods, and not a little of their food, from outside the region. Not only that, but Southern railroads and other establishments in the modern sector were increasingly controlled by outside capital. Profits that might have been reinvested in southern enterprise or helped to stimulate the local economy were drained off to the North. More important, decisions affecting the economic health of the region were made by men in Northern boardrooms who had a vested interest in maintaining it in its colonial status. Industrialization under the New South formula hurt the South, for the Redeemers were not simply advocating industrialization, they were arguing for laissez-faire capitalism and a changed way of life. This cultural treason could not be hidden by the nostalgic view of the Old South created in the 1880s to dissolve the Great Recantation in the syrup of romanticism.

Political conflict during the New South period consisted of sporadic insurgencies by the "wool-hat boys," frequently supported by the obsolescing planter aristocracy, against the Redeemer coalition and its alliance with the capitalist East. After twenty years of falling farm prices the agrarian uprising finally coalesced in the Populist movement and burst the bonds of the Democratic party in 1892 only to be decisively defeated in 1896 after a fatal decision to attempt fusion with the Democrats under the pennant of free silver held aloft by William Jennings Bryan. *Origins of the New South* presents the Populist movement in the tradition of *The Populist Revolt* of John D. Hicks as a rational, economic-interest political movement.[5] Contrary to Hicks, who slighted the southern branch of Populism and the issue of race relations within Populism, Woodward argued that Populism was stronger and more radical in the South than in the West and that Southern Populists made a sincere, though doomed, effort to effect a political alliance with blacks on the basis of economic self-interest. The ingrained racist feelings of the white Populist constituency contributed to the downfall of Populism.

As if determined not to be handicapped by the same problem, the progressives, who inherited the mantle of reform from the Populists, aided or acquiesced in disfranchisement and fashioned a brand of progressivism for whites only. Like progressivism outside the South, southern progressivism was urban and middle class. Though indigenous, with tinges of picturesque leadership and sectional rhetoric, it contained all the varieties of reform thought and action that were present on the national scene, and its leaders attracted business and finance as vigorously as did those anywhere. The problem with progressivism was that it did not go far enough, "it no more fulfilled the political aspirations and deeper needs of the mass of people than did the first New Deal administration." [6] The progressives carried over a strain of humanitarianism adapted from the tradition of patrician paternalism of the old ruling class. Nevertheless, the South that returned to national political power with Woodrow Wilson in 1913 after an absence of two generations was a very different region from the South that had attempted to establish its independence in the 1860s. A new middle-class leadership had guided it back into the mainstream of American life.

If one may apply labels without implying value judgments, *Origins of the New South* is a Beardian analysis. It is concerned throughout with the cynic's question: Who is in control and what are they after? It seems to accept at times the dualistic world view of the Populists and progressives themselves, a view in which the world is an arena of conflict between two contending forces: the classes versus the masses or business versus the people.[7] Similar views of the nature of conflict in the era of the Constitution, the early Republic, Jacksonian America, the secession crisis, Reconstruction, progressivism, and the New Deal have been destroyed or superseded during the last twenty years of historiography. To the extent that *Origins of the New South* is a Beardian analysis, and its deviations from the Beardian model will concern us later, one must wonder how much of it has survived the chippings and scrapings of scholars in the 1950s and 1960s.

There has been a gratifyingly large volume of monographic literature in the field since 1951, making this appear to be a case of the general preceding the particular. This is not unusual. As David H. Fischer reminds us, "The monographs do not commonly come first and the general interpretations second. Instead some master architect-no master builder-draws a rough sketch of a pyramid in the sand, and laborers begin to hew their stones to fit. Before many are made ready, the fashion suddenly changes—pyramids are out; obelisks are in."[8] The real surprise in this case is that the pyramid still stands. There has been no major challenge to *Origins of the New South*, except for the demurrers registered against its interpretation of trends in race relations, which are outside the concern of this essay, and certainly there has been no new master architect to offer a different design. The excellent essays by T. Harry Williams and Dewey W. Grantham Jr., the only two essays attempting a broad overview of

Southern politics between 1877 and 1913 to appear since the publication of *Origins of the New South*, follow the main furrows plowed by Woodward,[9] as do the most recent texts, *The South Since 1865* by John S. Ezell, *The South Since Appomattox* by Albert D. Kirwan and Thomas D. Clark, and *The American South* by Monroe Billington.[10] This is not to argue that the contributions to the field in the last twenty years have not been significant, for they have been. It is merely to say that they have been for the most part complementary and supplementary rather than contradictory.

The contradictions within *Origins of the New South* are nevertheless heightening in several important places. One of the most striking and original contributions of Professor Woodward in this book has been his revision of the story of the Compromise of 1877, the deal by which Rutherford B. Hayes was awarded the contested presidential election of 1876 by Southern forbearance in exchange for his promise to withdraw the last of the federal troops from South Carolina, Louisiana, and Florida and to appoint David M. Key to the postmaster generalship, thus bringing Reconstruction to a formal close. In a brilliant piece of detective work reported first in *Reunion and Reaction*[11] and then more briefly in *Origins of the New South*, Woodward uncovered an economic aspect of the deal and argued that the famous Wormley House bargain was a charade masking political and economic arrangements made in more discreet ways by representatives of Hayes and Whiggish Southern politicians. Among the most active of the "honest brokers" was Tom Scott, who stood to gain a federal subsidy for his faltering Texas and Pacific Railroad, a project in which Southern congressmen were interested for a variety of reasons.

One of the problems with this marvelous conspiracy, which captures in microcosm the Woodward view of the economically motivated Whiggish alliance of southern Redeemers and the capitalist East behind a movie-set façade of loyalty to the Old South, white supremacy, and home rule, is that though one can be sure the conspiracy existed and that Hayes gave his assurances through intermediaries that he would honor his end of the bargain, including "internal improvements of a national character," we do not know how committed Hayes was to specific economic aspects of the deal. Similarly, the link between the performance of the southern congressmen during the electoral crisis and the efforts of the Texas and Pacific lobby are inferential and circumstantial. After compiling a mass of evidence lending weight to the theme of persistent Whiggery, Thomas B. Alexander has expressed surprise that so few items in the Hayes papers refer to economic matters, and he suggests that given their backgrounds perhaps the southern congressmen would have behaved as they did in 1877 even without a conspiratorial bargain.[12] A recent biography of David M. Key by David M. Abshire, using Key papers not available to Woodward, reinforces Woodward's reconstruction of events, though Abshire understandably places more importance than Woodward on the necessity of Key's role.[13] Despite the new evidence, however, there are still gaps filled only by inference and doubt. The problem is cast into an even murkier state by the fact that Key had not been a Whig, though his political associates had, and by Professor Alexander's researches into the identity of antebellum Whigs which lead to the conclusion that there was little to differentiate Whig from Democratic voters except ideology.[14]

Whatever the social status of Whigs before the war, there have been some doubts expressed about Woodward's view of their role after the war. Lillian A. Pereyra's biography of James Lusk Alcorn describes a Whig who persisted by joining the Republican Party, a path taken by some other Whigs in Mississippi, particularly in the early days of Reconstruction.[15] Allen W. Moger, in his thorough reexamination of Virginia political history from the bourbons to Byrd, denies the validity of the persistent Whiggery theme in Virginia and argues that attitudes rather than old party affiliation motivated the men in control of the Virginia Democracy. This highlights the ambiguity in Woodward's account between Whiggery as an institutional loyalty and Whiggery as an aristocratic ideology, but Professor Moger's impression is sharply contradicted in the more detailed account of Virginia politics during the reconstruction era by Jack P. Maddex, Jr.[16] According to Maddex, former Whigs accounted for approximately half of the Conservative Party's leadership and, more important, the Conservative Party adapted itself to postwar realities by adopting the values which had characterized the Union Whigs before the war. Even though Maddex portrays the Conservatives as forward-looking modernizers rather than agents of the colonial power as in the Woodward account, and though he departs from Woodward in other small ways, he provides impressive confirmation of the major lines of interpretation in *Origins of the New South.*

A more substantial contradiction comes in the case of South Carolina where the Woodward thesis does not fit. According to William J.

Cooper, Jr., the South Carolina Bourbons were not former Whigs nor were they the agents of northern capital. Far from being new men, they were the offspring of planters. Political conflict in the Bourbon period, writes Cooper, did not take the form of class antagonism but was the outgrowth of other alignments, chiefly intrastate sectionalism.[17]

The import of Cooper's findings for the thesis of *Origins of the New South* is less clear because South Carolina may be a special case. As Cooper himself points out, the major reason for Whiggery not to persist in postwar South Carolina politics is that there was no significant Whig party before the war. In addition, Cooper's portrait of Tillmanism as something other than a class movement supports Woodward's view of Tillman as a charlatan in his role as a radical agrarian leader.

This leaves the question of whether South Carolina Bourbonism was in fact a restoration of the antebellum planter aristocracy or whether even in South Carolina the Civil War marked a significant interruption and redirection of the political structure. One statistical fact that historians should become aware of and attempt to explain is the dramatic shift in the occupational base of the political elite in the South between the 1850s and the 1880s. Ralph A. Wooster's painstaking quantitative studies of the power structure in the 1850s reveal that South Carolina was the most elitist of the southern states in terms of the economic status of its state officeholders.[18] Almost two-thirds of the South Carolina legislators in 1850 and in 1860 were planters or farmers, yet two-thirds of Cooper's sample of forty-three members of the postbellum elite was composed of lawyers, though the fathers of most of them had been planters. This implies a shift in the social basis of politics that is consistent with the views expressed in *Origins of the New South*. Future analyses should disclose whether or not Cooper is justified in taking the South Carolina Bourbons so much at their own evaluation in attributing their actions to a system of values deriving from a firm loyalty to the Old South, in attributing their defeat to rhetorical obsolescence rather than to clashes of class and economic interests, and in cleansing them of the charge of industrial Quislinghood by imputing innocence to the observation that "The Conservatives welcomed industry to South Carolina and worked to create a favorable atmosphere for its growth."[19]

The crucial question of continuity or discontinuity across the Civil War involves more than simply the antebellum political identity of the dominant element of the postbellum Democratic Party. Wilbur J. Cash, the South's foremost mythmaker, incorporated into his spellbinding evocation of the Piedmont mentality the New South propaganda's image of the planter's son becoming first a captain of cavalry and then after the war a captain of industry as the civilization of the Old South blended into the New South with scarcely a ripple in the social structure.[20] Woodward has dissented from this picture by implication in *Origins of the New South* and more explicitly in a recent publication.[21] William B. Hesseltine's study entitled *Confederate Leaders in the New South* takes some beginning steps toward a rigorous analysis of this problem by tracing the postwar careers of 656 Confederate officers.[22] His finding that they overwhelmingly held influential positions in society in the late nineteenth century is a welcome piece of evidence for the continuity school, but it is not a definitive answer for several reasons. We do not know much about the antebellum backgrounds or the Confederate officer corps as a group or about the degree of political dominance of Hesseltine's sample in the postbellum years or the extent to which the postbellum careers of Hesseltine's leaders are a fair sample of the postbellum careers of the surviving members of the antebellum elite. One of the next steps toward an answer to the continuity question should be a prosopographical study of the southern political elite in the 1880s. A comparison of the social origins and affiliations of the elites of the 1880s and the 1850s should tell us something about the transformation of the South in the era of the Civil War and lead us on to fruitful refinements of the question of continuity.

Woodward's mosaic of discontinuity includes an explication of the divided mind of the New South in which the dual loyalties of the Redeemer appear to be a more or less conscious exercise in Catoism. Recent histories such as those by Cooper and Moger, tend to take the Redeemer's professions of loyalty to the values of the Old South civilization more seriously than Woodward. This is also true of Paul Gaston's beautiful and authoritative intellectual analysis entitled *The New South Creed.*[23] Economic regeneration, national reconciliation, and racial adjustment were the major motifs of New South propaganda, in and around which played the idea of sectional self-determination and even dominance. Emulating the conquerors, the New South theorists thought, was the best way of getting rid of them. Though it is a major contribution to our understanding of the proponents of southern industrialization, Gaston's study is not primarily revisionist. He agrees with the judgment that the New South theorists served the region poorly by rationalizing industrialization on the disadvantageous terms set by northern capitalists, and he reinforces the perception of discontinuity by demonstrating how a revolutionary regime mobilizes the symbols of tradition in the service of change.

Those who resist change generally attract much less attention from historians than those who advocate it, particularly when the advocates win, and the South in the late nineteenth century is no exception to this rule. Clement Eaton takes a small step toward rectifying this oversight in his Lamar lectures, published as *The Waning of the Old South Civilization, 1860-1880's*, in which he places great emphasis upon "the tenacity of old forces and ideas rooted in the soil of the ante-bellum South."[24] A biography of Charles Colcock Jones, which is now in progress, should also add to our appreciation of the backward-looking elements in the New South.[25] That the plantation as a system of agriculture was not destroyed by the Civil War and emancipation is a well-known fact documented by Roger W. Shugg's study of Louisiana, reiterated by J. Carlyle Sitterson's study of the cane sugar industry, and incorporated by Woodward in *Origins of the New South*.[26] We are still in need of detailed studies of landownership, rural mobility patterns, and local economies and politics before we can be certain as to the effects of the Civil War upon southern social structures.

Robert L. Brandfon, in his study of the development of a rich plantation agriculture in the Yazoo-Mississippi Delta after the Civil War, contends that the postbellum planter, of whose origins we are still uncertain, differed from the antebellum planter in being conscious of the need for efficiency: "Underneath the romantic 'moonlight and magnolia' was a businesslike quest for profits."[27] Whether profit orientation was less a part of the planter's consciousness before the Civil War than after is an important topic for future scholarships,[28] but for the present Brandfon reminds us that the modernizers of the New South had an agricultural as well as an industrial policy. Brandfon thinks that both policies rested upon an unjustified and ultimately detrimental faith in the beneficence of outside capital, thus reinforcing the interpretive scheme of *Origins of the New South*.

In this regard Brandfon is in good company. Most of the state monographs done since 1951 reinforce much more than they revise about *Origins of the New South*. This is true of Albert D. Kirwan's narrative of Mississippi politics from 1876 to 1925 and of Allen J. Going's treatment of Alabama public life in the Bourbon period, both of which appeared soon after the publication of *Origins of the New South*.[29] Other than the deviations already discussed, Moger's account of Virginia throughout the late nineteenth century conforms to Woodward's patterns as do those of Raymond H. Pulley on Virginia, Joseph F. Steelman on North Carolina, James S. Ferguson on Mississippi, William W. Rogers on Alabama, and William I. Hair on Louisiana.[30] Aside from Sheldon Hackney, who tends to see the Populists in Alabama as much more opportunistic than does Woodward,[31] the only direct attempt to revise a part of the story of the southern uprising has been that mounted by Robert F. Durden in *The Climax of Populism*, in which he argues from a close examination of the evidence that the Populists at the national convention in 1896 were not duped by a conspiratorial leadership into fusion with Democrats.[32] Agreeing with Norman Pollack on at least this point, Durden suggests that fusion was not a desertion of principles but was logically seen by many Populists as the best next step toward general political reform. Despite the divergent results of their textual analyses, Durden and Woodward share a basic sympathy with Populism understood as an economic interest group composed of rational but oppressed farmers. That this interpretation has probably survived the brilliant revisionist rendering of Populism fashioned by Richard Hofstadter in *The Age of Reform* can be seen in the work of Theodore Saloutos.[33]

The neglect-of-the-losers rule has also applied to the other minority party, the Republicans. Allen W. Trelease's quantitative assessment of the identity of the scalawags lends credence to the assumption of continuity among poor whites in the upland South from Unionist sentiments in 1860 to scalawag Republicanism during Reconstruction to Independentism during the Gilded Age to populism during the 1890s.[34] This progression may be traced in the various monographs covering state politics in the late nineteenth century, and particularly in Moger and Rogers of the post-1951 books. Vincent P. De Santis and Stanley P. Hirshson overlap considerably in charting the ebb and flow of national Republican policy on the Southern Question.[35] Olive Hall Shadgett's study of Republicanism in Georgia underlines the fact that national Republicans did not drop their efforts to build a southern base in 1877.[36] Successive attempts to court white allies from various sectors of society to link with captive black Republican vote were all wrecked on the rocks of white supremacy. Mistreated, defrauded, manipulated, and abandoned though they were, black Republicans managed to play a significant role in southern politics well into the 1890s before disfranchisement and cynical apathy ushered in the era of "post office Republicanism" community during the last third of the century.

With blacks relegated to unthreatening political roles, the whites were free to divide, or so the theory went. One of the unsolved, even unposed, riddles of the twentieth-century Southern politics is why a two-party system did not develop after disfranchisement. The absence of an opposition party, of course, did not mean the absence of conflict, because fierce conflict did occur between personal followings or through intrastate sectionalism. The question really is why was there not enough strength or persistence in the factional alignments for one or more opposition parties to emerge. State parties have usually been organized from above in response to the needs of national politics, and the Republican Party certainly tried to create client organizations in the Southern states in the late nineteenth century. The frequent shifts in tactics and the taboo attaching to the party of Lincoln and Grant certainly encouraged Democratic loyalty among whites, and then Solid South allegiances were frozen into place by habit and the benefits of rotten-borough politics. That much of the answer is already in the literature. But when one considers that all the barriers, including an increasingly powerful black electorate, were overcome after World War II when the Southern Republican Party began to grow in response to the development of a heterogeneous urban culture, then one begins to suspect that there was something more than racism and habit underlying the one-party system. It may be that a homogeneity of economic interests and culture among whites was the real perpetuator of the Solid South. The argument that Democratic hegemony was supported by the voters because of the disproportionate power in national affairs accruing to long tenure rests, in fact, on the assumption that the electorate is not in conflict over the interests which such power is to serve, an assumptions that has been less and less valid since the New Deal.

Woodward's intuition that the Populist period resembled the era of the New Deal was not a distorted view. Both were dominated by economic depressions and experienced a reorientation of politics in which class had an increased influence on voter decisions. Since the publication of *Origins of the New South*, however, we have been made increasingly aware of the cultural component of Populist voting. Populists derived not only from inferior economic strata but from a rural segment of society that was being left behind by advancing technology and an increasingly urban society. They were defending a rural way of life, a culture, as well as a way of earning a living. Recent scholarship on politics in nineteenth-century America emphasizes the extent to which cultural divisions, and particularly ethnic identity, rather than class, served as the basis of political divisions.[37] The implications of this are at least two: that the success of Populism was inhibited to the extent that it was a departure from the more normal cultural bases of political divisions at the time, and secondly, that with the defeat of Populism and the success of disfranchisement there were few bases of political division left in the predominantly agricultural South except personal popularity, family loyalties, intrastate sectionalism, moral questions such as prohibition, and similar ephemeral alignments.

The result was that progressivism in the South took place within the Democratic Party. Since the publication of *Origins of the New South*, and since the path-marking essay by Arthur S. Link in 1946,[38] historians have been elaborating the idea that there was such an animal as southern progressivism.[39] State studies, such as those by Hackney, Pulley, Kirwan, and Moger, have added much, and there is an extensive journal literature,[40] but biographies have played the central role in developing our knowledge of southern progressivism. The list is long, including Hoke Smith by Dewey Grantham, James Stephen Hogg by Robert C. Cotner, George Washington Cable by Arlin Turner, Napoleon B. Broward by Samuel Proctor, Charles Brantley Aycock by Oliver H. Orr, Andrew Jackson Montague by William E. Larsen, Edward H. Crump of Memphis by William D. Miller, Josephus Daniels by Joseph L. Morrison, Josiah William Bailey by John R. Moore, James K. Vardaman by William F. Holmes, and Edgar Gardner Murphy by Hugh C. Bailey.[41] Together with some perceptive comments about southern progressivism in Robert H. Wiebe's stimulating interpretation, *The Search for Order*,[42] these works confirm the fact that the South experienced the full variety of reforms ranging from the businessman's drive for efficiency to proper middle-class concern for good government to hostility toward special economic interests, particularly toward those that were large and Yankee, to humanitarian concern for the wards of society and its

weaker members. Through all of this, no one has solved the paradox of how a region so different from the rest of the nation in its
history, its economic condition, and its social structure could produce a progressive movement differing in no special sense from the
national movement.

Other than a tendency to produce colorful and extravagant leaders, one of the few distinguishing traits of Southern progressivism
was its sponsorship of modernization with a proviso for economic
home rule. The progressive politician's charge that there was a Yankee conspiracy to keep the South in colonial bondage, which peeks
shyly from between the lines of *Origins of the New South*, has been
downgraded but not banished during the past two decades.[43] John F.
Stover's book, *The Railroads of the South, 1865-1900*, traces the
unrelenting extension of control of northern financial interests over
the southern railroad system,[44] and George W. Stocking explains the
inability of Birmingham to benefit from her natural advantages in
making steel by reference to the discriminatory basing-point system
used by United States Steel.[45]

On the other hand, David M. Potter, in an overlooked investigation,
argues that railroad rate differentials between sections existed from
the earliest time but that competition among railroads prevented ap-
preciable territorial discrimination until after 1920 when connect-
ing lines began to lose their independence and the Interstate Com-
merce Commission formalized the regional freight-rate structure
of the private associations.[46] The study by Calvin B. Hoover and
Benjamin U. Ratchford, *Economic Resources and Policies of the
South*, flatly states that high freight rates were never a major bar-
rier to the economic development of the South.[47] Much controversy surrounds the role of railroads in economic growth in the
nineteenth century,[48] and as the most powerful economic and political institutions of the period they will continue to interest historians. Recent studies, however, have tended to focus on issues other
than colonialism or to emphasize the contributions made by railroads to the development of the South.[49]

The matter on which there is the widest agreement at the present
is that, contrary to the utopian visions of the New South spokesmen,
no great leap or qualitative change occurred in the economy of the
South until after 1940.[50] The South remained an economy of low
incomes, labor-intensive enterprises, and primary industry. The question has been why so little change in that pattern?

In addition to the possibility of a colonialist conspiracy, several answers are available. William H. Nicholls has pinned the blame on the attitudes and values of southerners themselves in his book *Southern Traditions and Regional Progress*, a position disputed by William E. Laird and James R. Rinehart, who argue that capital stringency was the chief culprit in tying farmers to inefficient forms of agriculture and thus inhibiting industrialization.[51] Nicholls's colleague Anthony M. Tang, in an empirical investigation of development in twenty contiguous counties in the Georgia-South Carolina Piedmont, avoids that particular chicken-and-egg argument by raising another one. Applying an industrial-urban matrix approach to farm income differentials, Tang argues persuasively that the productivity of Southern farmers did not keep pace with the national average because of the lack of nearby industrial developments offering markets and part-time employment. Without the flexibility such opportunities provide, farm families are eventually unable to adapt successfully to changes in the agricultural market.[52]

The implication of this argument is that one-crop agriculture, the crop-lien system, and other malevolent institutions of the South would have collapsed as urban-industrial demands increased. Another implication is that insufficient out-migration hurt farm areas, and it may be as a hindrance to out-migration that the "passive" factor of values enters the picture, rather than as in the Nicholls formulation as a negative factor in entrepreneurial decisions. For instance, lacking local markets or employment opportunities in the late nineteenth century, southern farmers had the option to stay with the increasingly inadequate subsistence level of farming or to migrate to the city. It is difficult to explain their unwillingness to go to cities, as European immigrants by the millions were doing, unless the standard of living on the farm was actually better or farmers preferred a lower standard of living in the country to opportunity in a strange and alien city. As to the reasons for the scarcity of urban-industrial matrices in the South, one may trace the causes back to slavery, the plantation system, the topography of the South with it excellent interior river systems, or the commercial orientations of the original settlers. That is still an open question.[53] Meanwhile, we must find out more about the history of those urban centers that did exist.

Much more work is also needed on the problem of economic development, or the lack of it, and the process of economic growth in the period from the Civil War to World War II. Given all the barriers to growth-capital, destruction in the Civil War, investment opportunities elsewhere, the absence of urban centers and of a large urban middle class, low levels of education and public services, the scarcity of skilled labor, and all of the special problems faced by late-comers to the process of industrialization-it may be that historians have been asking the wrong question about growth. Nothing in the theory of regional economics would predict equilibrating capital flows, so perhaps we should not be seeking explanations for the slow rate of growth in the economy of the post-Civil War South but rather for the fact that it kept pace at all.[54] There has been, in fact, a general convergence of per capita incomes between the South and the nation, even though it has converged by fits and starts with a major reversal in the 1920s.[55] Furthermore, this has been accomplished despite the slow and late capital inflows from the North and despite the high rate of population growth. Any explanation must accommodate all these facts, and that is a great challenge.

Another great challenge stems from wondering about the causes for the instability of the Redeemer regimes that were defied by independent movements and torn by factional feuds even before they suffered the Populist revolt. Barrington Moore's analysis of sporadic rural political activities in England is very suggestive, whether or not it is correct, in tracing the source of unrest to the destruction of communal values by the enclosure movement. For Moore, in general, the evolution from noncommercial to commercial agriculture is the underlying cause of agrarian revolution.[56] Even though this concept is not at all foreign to American historians, it points to an unexplored source of tensions in the relationship between yeoman farmers and planters, a relationship about which we do not yet know enough either before or after the Civil War, nor do we know how it was changed by the war and its associated disruptions.

The outcome of any analysis of change across the Civil War very much depends upon one's conception of antebellum society. *Origins of the New South* employs a class and sectional analysis of the postbellum period that could comfortably interlock with the model of the Old South being developed by Eugene D. Genovese. Using concepts derived from Gramsci and Marx, Genovese posits a noncapitalistic, cohesive, and self-conscious planter aristocracy whose values infuse the entire society.[57] In the sequel, Woodward might have argued that the Redeemer regimes were unstable precisely because they were not based upon a popularly accepted system of values. The notables had made a much more rapid transition to capitalistic values, represented by the eastern alliance, than could the commoners, whose allegiance to old values is expressed in the desire to unite with the West. Without the controls provided by shared values, the Redeemers depended on fraud, emotional appeals to racial solidarity, and a low profile that would not excite voter opposition. But the economic crisis of the late 1880s shook loose the planter support from the Redeemer regimes and set the agrarian revolt on its course. As it gained momentum and drew more of the wool-hat set into its vortex, it spun leftward leaving disaffected planters in its wake.

Other starting points would lead to different outcomes. Morton Rothstein has suggested the utility of considering the Old South as a dual economy typical of developing nations.[58] Capitalistic planters, pursuing commercial profits through their links to distant markets, compose the modern sector; slaves and nonslaveholding whites who were only marginally concerned with production for the market make up the traditional sector. The linkage between the plantation, as both store and market, and the yeoman farmer completes a picture of a communal agriculture being practiced under the umbrella of an extensive commercial plantation system.[59] If this view is tenable, and there is much to recommend it, then one of the most far-reaching effects of the Civil War was to force both white and black farmers from the traditional sector into commercial agriculture where they were unable to survive. At the same time planters were shedding paternalistic roles to concentrate on their commercial functions. Whether one takes the cool, long view that this amounted to modernization and therefore was ultimately good, or whether one sees it as a devastating humans ordeal, one result is the same: agrarian protest. Populism may have been the cry of the rural masses for the recreation of a noncommercial community.

If historians are to place significance on the transition of poor whites from communal to commercial agriculture, we need to know a great deal more about Southern agricultural communities before and after the Civil War, and we particularly need social histories of black and white tenant farmers. In the sophisticated local studies that will produce the needed knowledge there must be a careful distinction made between "refuge farmers" and "venturing farmers," and this distinction should rest not upon the technology employed but upon the motive for farming.[60]

But until research produces new insights, the reality is that the pyramid still stands. *Origins of the New South* has survived relatively untarnished through twenty years of productive scholarship, including the eras of consensus and of the new radicalism, and remains the last of the Beardian syntheses. How can we explain this phenomenon? One possible answer is that Woodward is right about his period. Such an explanation has a certain elegance, and in this case even a bit of plausibility despite the notorious elusiveness of historical truth. The impeccable research that is evident in the volume has earned the respect of historians who have covered the same ground later, proving again that there is no substitute for knowing the primary sources. Nevertheless, correctness may be summarily dismissed as sufficient cause of longevity on the ground that revisionists have never been noticeable deterred by the absence of serious flaws in the body of knowledge they wished to revise.

There is also the matter of literary grace, present in full measure in *Origins of the New South*. Frederick Jackson Turner's famous essay is a pertinent example of the lasting power of an appealing prose style. Furthermore, Woodward is adept at synthesis and generalization and an absolute genius with the carefully qualified observation, a quality that has caused some difficulty when readers have not been as careful as the writer. Having granted all this, one still feels by instinct that some additional factor is at work and that it must be linked to Woodward's essential gift, which is a gift for irony.

The most arresting irony detected by Woodward is that America's most peculiar section, set apart from the nation by the very un-American experiences of guilt, defeat, and poverty, is not at all peculiar in the context of world history. For historians who characteristically ask how a people's experience helps to explain its behavior, there is an even more profound irony to be found in the high concentration of spread-eagle patriotism in the former Rebel states. It is another testimonial that suffering is not always ennobling and another demonstration of the fierceness with which outsiders adopt the myths and pretensions of the group to which they wish to belong. The touching intensity with which Johnny Cash simultaneously celebrates Indians, convicts, God, and the American flag is but a dramatic instance of the real irony of Southern history, the dual identity which is the result of a double history.

The national and the Southern identities are acquiring more and more common ground. Sensitive Americans today are learning what

Southerners learned a hundred years ago: that defeat is possible, that suffering is real, that failure to honor moral commitments brings retribution, that the past exacts its tribute from the present, that society is a complex and not very tractable set of human relationships and needs. The world of *Origins of the New South* is therefore at the same time familiar and instructive. It is a world of grandiose and pious pronouncements and tawdry performances in which big men fail and little men suffer. The message that emerges from *Origins of the New South* and from the whole body of Woodward's work is that history is a burden that weighs upon the present, structuring and restricting it. This is also a major theme of William Faulkner's work, particularly of *Absolom, Absolom; The Unvanquished*; and *The Sound and the Fury*. Though not as happy a message as the faith of the progressive historians nor as certain as that of the new radicals, it nevertheless harmonizes with some pervasive contemporary moods.

This is an age in which people attempt to find meaning in the meaninglessness of things. Historians, of course, are barred by the nature of their craft from dealing in the Absurd, or at least in the literary brand of it. Practitioners of the Absurd are engaged in dismantling appearance, eliding the boundary between illusion and reality, demonstrating the essential lack of pattern and predictability beneath our commonsense understanding of the world. Historians, on the other hand, begin with the assumption that the past is a patternless jumble of phenomena on which the historian must impose his own order or one that he may find lying about. The models currently available for borrowing are not very reassuring. When one turns to our literature he finds McMurphy, Yossarian, Herzog, Portnoy, the Graduate, Norwood, and a long stream of nonheroes. As Charles A. Reich contends in *The Greening of America*, the modern American feels so powerless that he is unable to conceive of a hero who can alter fate by taking action. Thus, Humphrey Bogart in *Casablanca* may be the last American hero.[61]

As the whimsical popularity of cartoon heroes implies, we have turned Carlyle upside down. When Charles Portis wrote a story of real gumption and guts, he called it *True Grit*, set it in the nineteenth century, and made it a parody of a true-life reminiscence. David Douglas Duncan's portfolio of photographs of frontline soldiers in Vietnam, for another example, is entitled *War Without Heroes*.[62] The young, the mobile, and the metropolitan, having lost their sense of original sin and their belief in transcendent values, evidently find it difficult to imagine a hero. How ironic in such a time that we should still find compatibility in literature that documents original sin and assumes transcendent values. This springs in part from the South's old role as foil and counterpoint for national moods, but it comes in part also from the link between the nonheroic sensibility of the present and the theme in Woodward and Faulkner of the individual being bullied about by fate, crushed by outside forces over which he has no control, or victimized by conspiracies of the strong. Populists and modern nonheroes have in common the fact that they are victims, yet they frequently enlist our sympathies and enlarge our vision of humanity by their willingness to struggle.

There are few heroes in *Origins of the New South*, and the few who do appear are of the tragic variety. Tom Watson is such a faulted hero, if one has compassion and empathy enough to understand him and those for whom he spoke. A hero while losing, he was transformed by defeat into a successful villain, only to be consumed by his own hatred. It is a theme worthy of William Faulkner's tragic vision of the South, a vision shared by Woodward to an extent stopping somewhat short of fatalism. *Origins of the New South* would provide a familiar context for Faulkner's characters: the decaying Sartoris family suffering from the sin of slavery, the opportunistic Compsons doomed for their materialistic rejection of the land, patrician Coldfields with enlightened racial views, poor whites like Hope Hampton who behave with honor despite racial prejudice, blacks who achieve dignity and respect like Lucas Beauchamp and Dilsey, and of course, the Snopes tribe, filtering into the growing towns from the backcountry, taking control and losing out, transforming the South for better or worse, but always struggling.

Woodward's sensibility is both Beardian and Faulknerian, and the combination of the two is the source of the continuing appeal of *Origins of the New South*. Richard Hofstadter observed that, "As practiced by mature minds, history forces us to be aware not only of complexity but of defeat and failure: it tends to deny that high sense of expectation, that hope of ultimate and glorious triumph, that sustains good combatants. There may be comfort in it still. In an age when so much of our literature is infused with nihilism, and other social disciplines are driven toward narrow positivistic inquiry, history may remain the most humanizing among the arts."[63] Woodward is certainly a humanizing historian, one who recognizes both the likelihood of failure and the necessity of struggle. It is the profound ambiguity that makes his work so interesting. Like the myth of Sisyphus, *Origins of the New South* still speaks to our condition. And who knows? Perhaps one day we will get that rock to the top of the hill. But, having learned my skepticism at the master's knee, I doubt it.

Notes

1. Woodward, *Origins of the New South, 1877-1913* (Baton Rouge, La., 1951).
2. For an intelligent brief discussion of the New South school, see Paul M. Gaston, "The New South,'" in Arthur S. Link and Rembert W. Patrick, eds., *Writing Southern History: Essays in Historiography in Honor of Fletcher M. Green* (Baton Rouge, La., 1965), 321-26.
3. Thompson, *The New South: A Chronicle of Social and Industrial Evolution* (New Haven, Conn., 1919), 203-4
4. Ibid., 192.
5. Hicks, *The Populist Revolt: A History of the Farmers' Alliance and the People's Party* (Minneapolis, Minn., 1931).
6. Woodward, *Origins of the New South*, 395.
7. That Charles Beard's interpretation of the motivations of the makers of the Constitution was actually pluralistic is one of the points of Lee Benson's excellent analysis in his book, *Turner and Beard: American Historical Writing Reconsidered* (Glencoe, Ill. 1960), but there are senses in which Marx was not a Marxist either. There is a rich literature on the historiography of Beardianism: Cushing Strout, *The Pragmatic Revolt in American History: Carl Becker and Charles Beard* (New Haven, Conn., 1958); Robert A. Skotheim, *American Intellectual Histories and Historians*, (Princeton, N. J., 1966); David W. Noble, *Historians Against history: The Frontier Thesis and the National Covenant in American Historical Writing Since 1830* (Minneapolis, Minn., 1965); Richard Hofstadter, *The Progressive Historians; Turner, Beard, Parrington* (New York, 1968); Charles Crowe, "The Emergence of Progressive history," *Journal of the History of Ideas*, 27 (January-March 1966), 109-24.
8. Fischer, *Historians' Fallacies: Toward a Logic of Historical Thought* (New York, Evanston, and London, 1970), 5.
9. Grantham, *The Democratic South* (Athens, Ga., 1963), and Williams, *Romance and Realism in Southern Politics* (Athens, Ga., 1961).
10. Ezell, *The South Since 1865* (New York and London, 1963); Clark and Kirwan, *The South Since Appomattox: A Century of Regional Change* (New York, 1967; Billington, *The American South* (New York, 1971).
11. Woodward, *Reunion and Reaction: The Compromise of 1877 and the End of Reconstruction* (Boston, 1951).
12. Alexander, "Persistent Whiggery in the Confederate South, 1860-1877," *Journal of Southern History,* 27 (August 1961), 305-29.
13. Abshire, *The South Rejects a Prophet: The Life of Senator D. M. Key, 1824-1900* (New York, Washington, and London, 1967).
14. Alexander et al., "The Basis of Alabama's Ante-Bellum Two-Party System," *Alabama Review*, 19 (October 1966), 243-76; Alexander et al., "Who Were the Alabama Whigs?" ibid., 16 (January 1963), 5-19; Grady McWhiney, "Were the Whigs a Class Party in Alabama?" *Journal of Southern History*, 23 (November 1957), 510-22.

15. Pereyra, *James Lusk Alcorn, Persistent Whig* (Baton Rouge, 1966); David Donald, "The Scalawags in Mississippi Reconstruction," *Journal of Southern History*, 10 (November 1944), 447-60; Allen W. Trelease, "Who Were the Scalawags?" ibid., 29 (November 1963), 445-68; William C. Harris, "A Reconsideration of the Mississippi Scalawags," *Journal of Mississippi History*, 32 (February 1970), 3-42.

16. Moger, *Virginia: Bourbonism to Byrd, 1870-1925* (Charlottesville, 1968); Maddex, *The Virginia Conservatives, 1867-1879: A Study in Reconstruction Politics* (Chapel Hill, N.C., N.C., 1970).

17. Cooper, *The Conservative Regime: South Carolina, 1877-1890* (Baltimore, Md., 1968).

18. Wooster, *The People in Power: Courthouse and Statehouse in the Lower South, 1950-1860* (Knoxville, Tenn., 1969).

19. Cooper, *Conservative Regime*, 120.

20. Cash, *The Mind of the South* (New York, 1941), 205.

21. Woodward, "W.J. Cash Reconsidered," *New York Review of Books*, 13 (December 4, 1969), 28-34.

22. Hesseltine, *Confederate Leaders in the New South* (Baton Rouge, 1950).

23. Gaston, *The New South Creed: A Study in Southern Mythmaking* (New York, 1970).

24. Eaton, *The Waning of the Old South Civilization, 1860-1880's* (Athens, Ga., 1968).

25. J. William Berry of Princeton University is studying Jones for his Ph.D. dissertation under the direction of Arthur S. Link. See also Hugh C. Davis, "An Analysis of the Rationale of Representative Conservative Alabamians, 1874-1914" (Ph.D. dissertation, Vanderbilt University, 1964).

26. Shugg, "Survival of the Plantation System in Louisiana," *Journal of Southern History,* 3 (August 1937), 311-25; Sitterson, *Sugar Country: The Cane Sugar Industry in the South 1753-1950* (Lexington, Ky., 1953).

27. Brandfon, *Cotton Kingdom of the New South: A History of the Yazoo Mississippi Delta from Reconstruction to the Twentieth Century* (Cambridge, Mass., 1967), viii.

28. See Robert E. Gallman, "Self-Sufficient in the Cotton Economy of the Antebellum South," *Agricultural History*, 44 (January 1970), 5-23. This entire issue, edited by William N. Parker, is devoted to papers on "The Structure of the Cotton Economy of the Antebellum South" and is available in book form from the Agricultural History Society.

29. Kirwan, *Revolt of the Rednecks: Mississippi Politics, 1876-1925* (Lexington, Ky., 1951); Going, *Bourbon Democracy in Alabama, 1874-1890* (University, Ala., 1951).

30. Pulley, *Old Virginia Restored: An Interpretation of the Progressive Impulse, 1870-1930* (Charlottesville, 1968); Steelman, "The Progressive Era in North Carolina, 1884-1917" (Ph.D. dissertation, University of North Carolina, 1955) Steelman, "Vicissitudes of Republican Party Politics: The Campaign of 1892 in North Carolina," *North Carolina Historical Review*, 43 (October 1966), 430-41; Steelman, "Republican Party Strategists and the Issue of Fusion with Populists in North Carolina, 1893-1894," ibid., 47 (July 1970), 244-69; Rogers, *The One-Gallused Rebellion: Agrarianism in Alabama, 1865-1896* (Baton Rouge, La. 1970); Hair, *Bourbonism and Agrarian Protest: Louisiana Politics, 1877-1900* (Baton Rouge, La., 1969).

31. Hackney, *Populism to Progressivism in Alabama* (Princeton, N.J., 1969). Helen G. Edmonds, in *The Negro and Fusion Politics in North Carolina, 1894-1901* (Chapel Hill, N.C., 1951), also exposes the opportunism of the Populist racial policies, but otherwise the fusion forces appear progressive in her pages.

32. Durden, *The Climax of Populism: The Election of 1896* (Lexington, Ky., 1965).
33. Hofstadter, *The Age of Reform: From Bryan to F.D.R.* (New York, 1955); Saloutos, "The Professors and the Populists," *Agricultural History*, 40 (October 1966), 235-54; and Saloutos, *Farmer Movements in the South, 1865-1933* (Berkeley, Cal., 1960). For an extensive bibliography on populism, with an introduction discussing the state of the field, see Sheldon Hackney, ed., *Populism: The Critical Issues* (Boston, 1971).
34. Trelease, "Who Were the Scalawags?"
35. DeSantis, *Republicans Face the Southern Question: The New Departure Years, 1877-1897* (Baltimore, Md., 1959); Hirshson, *Farewell to the Bloody Shirt: Northern Republicans and the Southern Negro, 1877-1893* (Bloomington, Ind., 1962).
36. Shadgett, *The Republican Party in Georgia from Reconstruction Through 1900* (Athens, Ga., 1964).
37. Paul Kleppner, *The Cross of Culture: A Social Analysis of Midwestern Politics, 1850-1900* (New York, 1970): Lee Benson, *The Concept of Jacksonian Democracy: New York as a Test Case* (Princeton, N.J., 1961).
38. Link, "The Progressive Movement in the South, 1870-1914," *North Carolina Historical Review*, 23 (April 1946) 172-95.
39. For instance, see Anne Firor Scott, "A Progressive Wind from the South, 1906-1913," *Journal of Southern History*, 29 (February 1963), 53-70; Herbert J. Doherty, Sr., "Voices of Protest from the New South, 1875-1910," *Mississippi Valley Historical Review*, 42 (June 1955), 45-66; William D. Miller, *Memphis During the Progressive Era, 1900-1917* (Memphis, Tenn., 1957); and Pulley, *Old Virginia Restored.*
40. See the bibliographical essay by Dewey W. Grantham Jr., in Link and Patrick, eds., *Writing Southern History*, 410-44.
41. Grantham, *Hoke Smith and the Politics of the New South* (Baton Rouge, La., 1958); Cotner, *James Stephen Hogg: A Biography* (Austin, 1959); Turner, *George W. Cable: A Biography* (Durham, N.C., 1956); Proctor, *Napoleon Bonaparte Broward: Florida's Fighting Democrat* (Gainesville, 1950); Orr, *Charles Brantley Aycock* (Chapel Hill, N.C., 1961); Larsen, *Montague of Virginia: The Making of a Southern Progressive* (Baton Rouge, La., 1965); Miller, *Mr. Crump of Memphis* (Baton Rouge, La., 1964); Morrison, *Josephus Daniels Says...: An Editor's Political Odyssey from Bryan to Wilson and F.D.R., 1894-1913* (Chapel Hill, N.C., 1962); *Josephus Daniels: The Small-d Democrat* (Chapel Hill, N.C., 1966); Moore, *Senator Josiah William Bailey of North Carolina: A Political Biography* (Durham, N.C., 1968); Holmes, *The White Chief: James Kimble Vardaman* (Baton Rouge, La., 1970); Bailey, *Edgar Gardner Murphy: Gentle Progressive* (Coral Gables, Fl., 1968) *Also see Bailey, Liberalism in the New South: Southern Social Reform and the Progressive Movement* (Coral Gables, Fl., 1960).
42. Weibe, *The Search for Order, 1877-1920* (New York, 1967).
43. Clarence H. Danhof, "Four Decades of Thought on the South's Economic Problems," in Melvin L. Greenhut and W. Tate Whitman, eds., *Essays in Southern Economic Development* (Chapel Hill, N.C., 1964), 7-68.
44. Stover, *The Railroads of the South, 1865-1900* (Chapel Hill, N.C., 1955). The best monograph documenting the impact of railroads on politics in James F. Doster, *Railroads in Alabama Politics, 1875-1914* (University, Ala., 1957).
45. Stocking, *Basing Point Pricing and Regional Development: A Case Study of the Iron and Steel Industry* (Chapel Hill, N.C., 1954). See also Justin Fuller, "History of the Tennessee Coal, Iron and Railroad Company, 1852-1907" (Ph.D. dissertation, University of North Carolina, 1966).

46.   Potter, "The Historical Development of Eastern-Southern Freight Rate Relationships," *Law and Contemporary Problems*, 12 (Summer 1947), 416-48.

47.   Hoover and Ratchford, *Economic Resources and Policies of the South* (New York, 1951), 78.

48.   See Robert W. Fogel, *Railroads and American Economic Growth: Essays in Economic History* (Baltimore, 1964); Albert Fishlow, *American Railroad and the Transformation of the Ante-Bellum Economy* (Cambridge, Mass., 1965); and Peter D. McClelland, "Railroads, American Growth, and the New Economic History: A Critique," *Journal of Economic History,* 28 (March 1968), 102-23.

49.   Leonard P. Curry, *Rail Routes South: Louisville's Fight for the Southern Market, 1865-1872* (Lexington, Ky., 1969); Maury Klein, *The Great Richmond Terminal: A Study in Businessmen and Business Strategy* (Charlottesville, 1970); and Klein, "The L & N Railroad and the South, 1865-1893: A Case Study in Regional Development," paper presented at the annual meeting of the Southern Historical Association, Louisville, Kentucky, November 11-14, 1970.

50.   Thomas D. Clark, in *The Emerging South* (New York, 1961), suggests that the crucial changes began with the failure of the cotton crop in 1921 but agrees, in *Three Paths to the Modern South: Education, Agriculture, and Conservation* (Athens, Ga., 1965), that no economic revolution had yet occurred in 1940. This question can be most authoritatively followed in George B. Tindall, *The Emergence of the New South, 1913-1945* (Baton Rouge, 1967). Gerald D. Nash provides an informed guide to existing literature and future possibilities in "Research Opportunities in the Economic history of the South After 1880," *Journal of Southern History*, 32 (August 1966), 308-24.

51.   Nicholls, *Southern Tradition and Regional Progress* (Chapel Hill, N.C., 1960); Laird and Rinehart, "Deflation, Agriculture, and Southern Development," *Agricultural History*, 42 (April 1968), 115-24.

52.   Tang, *Economic Development in the Southern Piedmont, 1860-1950: Its Impact on Agriculture* (Chapel Hill, N.C., 1958).

53.   A suggestive essay on antebellum urbanization in the South is provided by Julius Rubin, "Urban Growth and Regional Development," in David T. Gilchrist, ed., *The Growth of Seaport Cities, 1790-1825* (Charlottesville, 1967), 3-21.

54.   See, for instance Harry W. Richardson, *Regional Economics: Location Theory, Urban Structure and Regional Change* (London, 1969), 330.

55.   Richard A. Easterlin, "Interregional Differences in Per Capita Income, Population, and Total Income, 1840-1950," in National Bureau of Economic Research, *Trends in the American Economy in the Nineteenth Century: Studies in Income and Wealth* (Princeton, 1960), 73-140.

56.   Barrington Moore Jr., *Social Origins of Dictatorship and Democracy: Lord and Peasant in the Making of the Modern World* (Boston, 1966).

57.   Genovese, *The Political Economy of Slavery: Studies in the Economy and Society of the Slave South* (New York, 1965); Genovese, *The World the Slaveholders Made: Two Essays in Interpretation* (New York, 1969).

58.   Rothstein, "The Antebellum South as a Dual Economy: A Tentative Hypothesis," *Agricultural History*, 41 (October 1967), 373-82.

59.   There is an extensive and illuminating literature on this unresolved set of issues. The best beginning point now is William N. Parker, ed., "The Structure of the Cotton Economy of the Antebellum South," *Agricultural History*, 44 (January 1970), 1-165. See also Lewis E. Atherton, *The Southern Country Store, 1800-1860* (Baton Rouge, 1949); Frank L. Owsley, *Plain Folk of the Old South* (Baton Rouge, 1949); and Fabian Linden, "Economic Democracy in the Slave South: An Appraisal of Some Recent Views," *Journal of Negro History*, 31 (April 1946), 140-89.

60.   Wayne C. Rohrer and Louis H. Douglas, *The Agrarian Transition in America: Dualism and Change* (Indianapolis, 1967); Douglas C. North, "Location Theory and Regional Economic Growth," *Journal of Political Economy*, 63 (June 1955), 243-58; John Friedman and William Alonso, eds., *Regional Development and Planning: A Reader* (Cambridge, Mass., 1964). A step forward in the increasing sophistication of local studies is made by George C. Rogers Jr., *The History of Georgetown County, South Carolina* (Columbia, S.C., 1970).

61.   Reich, *The Greening of America* (New York, 1970), 146. Reich himself is a prophetic hero of the universal variety described by Joseph Campbell in *The Hero with a Thousand Faces* (New York, Evanston, and London, 1949), who suffers separation, travels in the land of death overcoming obstacles, and returns to give to mankind a redemptive message providing new sources of power. But that is a different kind of hero.

62.   Duncan, *War Without Heroes* (New York, 1970.

63.   Hofstadter, *Progressive Historians*, 466.

3

"*Origins of the New South* in Retrospect" Thirty Years Later[1]

The Jubilee year for C. Vann Woodward's *Origins of the New South* was 2001. We learn from Leviticus 25: 1-23 that God, speaking to the children of Israel through Moses, prescribed that every seventh year should be a Sabbath year, during which the fields would lie fallow; after a week of Sabbath years there should be a Jubilee year in which debts are to be forgiven, ancestral lands restored, slaves released from bondage, and freedom proclaimed throughout the land.

I exercised my privilege as a liberated bondman during Jubilee to return home to my ancestral topic, only to discover how much the topic has changed since my last visit. Thirty-two years ago, in 1971, I was invited to deliver a paper at the spring meeting of the Organization of American Historians evaluating *Origins* as it celebrated its twentieth birthday and as a second edition was being published.[2] Being young and foolish, and wanting a trip to New Orleans, I accepted. I was on leave that academic year doing research on the civil rights movement. My notes on civil rights continue to gather mold, of course, and I am still trying to figure out how such a revolutionary book as *Origins* could have gone a full generation without attracting major revisionists. It was not that historians had ignored the era, as confirmed by Charles B. Dew's 110-page critical essay on authorities that was included in the second edition. Woodward himself was a little surprised that no fundamental challenge had arisen, but in his disarming intellectual memoir, *Thinking Back: The Perils of Writing History*, he agreed with me that in 1971 the "pyramid still

Reprinted by permission of Louisiana State University Press from *Origins of the New South, 1877-1913, Fifty Years Later: The Continuing Influence of a Historic Classic*, edited by John B. Boles and Bethany Johnson. Copyright 2003 by Louisiana State University Press.

stands."[3] Most significantly, he made no revisions for the second edition of *Origins*; he simply added a brief foreword.

What accounts for the staying power of *Origins*? Thirty years ago I somewhat facetiously suggested that the longevity of *Origins* might be traced to the correctness of Woodward's interpretation, but I dismissed that possibility as unlikely because soundness of argument had never deterred critics before. Instead, I suggested that the tragic story that Woodward told resonated in an era of disillusionment, when the shock troops of multiple social justice movements had produced a society at war with itself at home, just as it found itself fighting an unpopular and unwinnable war abroad—a war without heroes, just as *Origins* attacked the meta-narrative of American exceptionalism, the national myth that all problems have solutions, that the solutions are to be found in the application of human reason and technology, and that the United States, as the world's exemplar of freedom through democracy, is so blessed that progress and success ore inevitable.

The resilience of this national self-image is amazing. It has not only been revived in recent years, but it colors the way we see even the Gilded Age. Yes, there was the genocide of the Native Americans, the disastrous desertion of recently freed slaves in the South by the federal government and the Northern public, the corruption of affairs by politicians of Lilliputian stature and business tycoons with morals to match, the brutality of the Robber Barons, the exploitation of immigrants and blue-collar laborers, the wretched lives lived by the "other half," the subjugation of colonial populations, and the exclusion from immigration of non-European peoples. Nevertheless, if you squint properly, the Gilded Age can be seen as a continuation of the inevitable march of progress: there was the romance of rapid urbanization and industrialization, the taming of the West, the creation of great American fortunes, a dramatically rising standard of living, the emergence of the United States as a world power, and the rise of Progressivism, a reform movement aimed at checking all of the abuses mentioned above. If you keep your eyes fixed on the nation, and ignore real people, it is a heroic success story.

For the South, however, the story was different; there was unrelieved poverty, agricultural depression, social dislocation, and racial friction. Promising a new Eden in which Southerners would live with modern comforts without having to give up their traditional values, the New South crusade produced a lot of running hard just to stay in place—a place at the bottom of the income, wealth, and power distribution. Nevertheless, the conventional view of the period 1877-1913 that Woodward replaced was pretty much the version that would have been written by Henry W. Grady or the most self-serving conservative Redeemer, full of hope, progress, and the justification of white supremacy. In contrast, Woodward's story in *Origins* was a time and place in which defeat, poverty, and gloomy prospects were everyday realities for a lot of Americans. His sense of historical contingency and the likelihood of failure spoke to the crisis of confidence that began in America in the mid-1960s and lasted until the mid-1990s.

From our current vantage point in the Jubilee year, it is possible to see patterns that were not so evident in 1951 or even 1971. We can see, for instance, that Woodward, the genteel controversialist, was constantly probing the past for lessons that would speak to the most fundamental issues of the current day: the politics of scarcity, racial justice, and the dangers of national self-righteousness. It is a mistake, Woodward was saying in *Origins*, to assume that our national story flowed continuously forward without conflict or serious disruption, encapsulated in the myths of innocence, success, and affluence. Woodward was engaged in the old game of using the history of the South to instruct the nation.

Though he did not specifically object to my "malaise" theory to explain the bulletproof nature of *Origins* through its first twenty years, his own explanation was that there was a different sense in which the times favored his theme of discontinuity across the Civil War. Because the 1950s and 1960s witnessed huge discontinuities in Southern life, he reasoned, the profession was willing to entertain the idea that the Civil War had occasioned a similar fundamental break with the past.

To use a Woodwardian technique against the master, I need only point out that as change in the South has accelerated over the succeeding thirty years, occasioning greater and greater distance between its present reality and its mythic past, the ranks of the naysayers to the Woodwardian discontinuity theme have also swelled, contrary to what should have happened if his explanation were correct. My own current guess about the delayed-action doubters is that Woodward had done such a prodigious amount of archival research for *Origins* that it took a long time for even a brash challenger to master the primary sources in some comfortable niche sufficiently to mount a credible challenge.

However charmed the youth of *Origins*, its adulthood since 1971 has been productively normal. Historians have been swinging their sledgehammers from various angles with mounting ferocity. Consequently, *Origins* is dented, discolored, tattered, and torn, but it is still there, still the mandatory starting point for any serious study of the South between 1877 and 1913. On the other hand, there are now alternative opinions on every major question. Rather than having an uncontested narrative, we have rubble heaps of fascinating arguments dotting the countryside. Woodward relished it. Let me point out the major ruins and historical sites.

Origins opens with a synopsis of *Reunion and Reaction*, Woodward's economic conspiracy theory of the Compromise of 1877.[4] We still lack definitive evidence, but the consensus seems to be that even though the conspiracy that Woodward unearthed actually existed, it is doubtful that it had a decisive effect on the outcome of the crisis because there were straightforward political incentives that were strong enough by themselves to have led Democrats to allow Rutherford B. Hayes to be sworn in as president.[5]

On the crucial question of whether continuity or discontinuity best describes the connection between the Old and New South, there is convincing evidence that landownership did not change rapidly, nor did the agricultural basis of the economy. Furthermore, many of the New South entrepreneurs derived from the elite antebellum class and even continued to pay homage to the older values and aspirations.[6] Woodward responded in *Thinking Back*, and many historians agree, that even among persisting planters and other members of the elite in the New South there was a major shift in mentality or outlook. The ethos of the 1880s and 1890s was markedly different from that of the 1850s. Planters may have been engaged in their old tasks of growing staple crops for distant markets, but their plantations were organized differently, with tenant farmers and sharecroppers. Their managerial task was therefore different, and they displayed a new businesslike mind-set. Furthermore, economic roles were increasingly complex, so that planters were not only managers and landlords but also bankers and merchants, as well perhaps as lawyers in town and even promoters of the local cotton mill.[7]

Woodward's Redeemers were an unattractive lot, selfish and manipulative, but the more historians look at them, the more they seem to be representative of the cross section of humanity. Many were venal and self-serving, but there were those who thought they were pursuing their community's best interests as well as their own through industrialization. They look no worse than antebellum planters, but that was the class that got the South into a disastrous war.

No one dissents from the idea that race was a central theme of the period, but increasingly historians are stressing the degree to which African Americans were active in their own behalf, resisting the fraud, intimidation, and violence that eventually led to their disfranchisement and segregation. This is a missing perspective in *Origins*. That there was widespread segregation, even going back to the antebellum period, is increasingly clear, some of it even initiated by freedpeople to assure access to public space, but it is also clear that race etiquette and roles were in flux throughout the period and that patterns of race relations varied enormously from one community to another. That was not changed decisively until the 1890s and 1990s by Jim Crow legislation that created a fixed, uniform, and universal system rooted in the law.[8]

Woodward has conceded that the Populists were not as altruistically egalitarian with regard to race as he implied in *Origins*. On the other hand, in the context of the times, even the segregated political pragmatism of the Populists was an advanced stance. Arguments still rage about which class or group was most responsible for disfranchisement, the conservative elite or the reform Democrats. Of that particular crime, the Populists were not guilty.[9]

No one today agrees with Richard Hofstadter's thesis in *The Age of Reform* that cast the Populists as backward-looking and socially marginal people, characterized by various unlovely traits.[10] In fact, the dominant treatment of Populism by Lawrence Goodwyn is more Woodwardian than Woodward himself, portraying the Populists not only as rationally aggrieved for economic reasons but as the last best hope for an effective democracy. Historians here and there suggest that the Populists may not have been the proto-New Dealers they are often portrayed as being, but that, at the moment, is a minority voice.[11] There are scholars, however, who disagree with Woodward about fusion with the Democrats in 1896. Even though it did not work out well in practice, these historians think fusion with the reform wing of the Democratic Party was a logical political step rather than a capitulation by the fainthearted.

We are still pondering the big question of why it took so long for the South to modernize. Woodward's answer was that the South became a colonial economy after the Civil War and that Northern capitalists had an economic self-interest in keeping it that way. Some historians, however, are not at all sure that differential freight rates, for instance, had anything to do with slow industrialization. Some, in fact, wonder whether the rate of modernization in the South cannot be explained by the depth of poverty after the Civil War, by the unusual difficulties experienced by latecomers to the process of modernization, and especially by uncongenial cultural values growing out of plantation society and persisting across the Civil War. Furthermore, though the South did not close the economic gap appreciably during the period from Reconstruction to World War I, perhaps it is remarkable that it did not fall further behind, because the nation was making gigantic strides forward in industrialization and urbanization.[12]

The voices of women are inaudible in *Origins*, but a new soundtrack is being added at a great rate. Those female voices are not only found singing harmony on the front porch during family songfests; they are intruding into the public sphere, as in Glenda Elizabeth Gilmore's astute study of North Carolina, *Gender and Jim Crow*.[13]

Origins is focused relentlessly on the public sphere, on the actions of leaders and followers in political and economic arenas. For an appreciation of how ordinary people lived and the popular culture they spawned, one should read *The Promise of the New South*, by Edward Ayers, a masterful telling from multiple points of view of the story of the South in the same period covered by *Origins*. Ayers finds more optimism in the New South than did Woodward, but in general his portrait is complementary rather than contradictory.[14]

The best guide to these various challenges and emendations is Woodward himself in *Thinking Back*. John Herbert Roper provides sympathetic biographical context and a comprehensive analysis in *C. Vann Woodward, Southerner*, as well as a sampling of the controversies in *C. Vann Woodward: A Southern Historian and His Critics*. Howard N. Rabinowitz, in *The First New South, 1865-1920*, and John B. Boles, in *The South Through Time: A History of an American Region*, can also be trusted as pathfinders through the Woodwardian thickets.[15]

One wonders, of course, what the subtext of *Origins* would be if Woodward were writing today. The perspective would necessarily be different because the South is different. It has almost caught up with the non-South in income; it has disproportionate political power;

and it watches with wry amusement as so many things Southern attain a certain national cachet, from country music and NASCAR to the pampered self, as pictured in the magazine *Southern Living*.

More important, what could the story of the South in the late nineteenth century have to teach the nation in the wake of the terrorism of September 11, 2001, a nation shaken in its infatuation with materialism and radical individualism, a nation newly alerted to lasting values and to the importance of communities of mutual sacrifice, a nation conscious at last perhaps of the dangers of tolerating vast disparities in wealth and well-being either within American society or between first world and third world peoples?

I think the lesson should be that the costs of keeping the dispossessed down are significant and are borne by society as a whole. Local elites in the South, with a vested interest in keeping the labor force docile and cheap, myopically used racism to enforce conformity. The result was a society with an extremely limited ability to change itself or to respond adequately to an increasingly complex world. Education, transportation, public health, high-yield agriculture, and public services of all kinds received inadequate investment. Massive out-migration in the twentieth century was the marker of a failed public philosophy. It was not until the federal government put military bases and defense plants in the South during World War II that the Southern economy achieved self-sustaining growth and began to close the gap with the rest of the nation in such indices as per capita income, not to mention education, health, and other indicators of "life chances." Outsiders had to instigate the economic change, just as they were crucial to the success of the efforts of black Southerners to achieve full citizenship. The lesson is that when public policy is captured by an elite and focused on the policies that serve the short-term interests of that elite, the long-term effect is that everyone suffers—even the favored elites. That is what happened in the South.

When I wrote my original assessment of Woodward's masterpiece in 1971, I could not have known that Woodward's greatest work was behind him. In the category of "great" I would place the books that restructured our way of thinking about the history of the South, especially for the period from the end of Reconstruction to World War I: *Tom Watson, Agrarian Rebel*; *Reunion and Reaction*; *Origins of the New South*; *The Strange Career of Jim Crow*; and the essays collected in *The Burden of Southern History*.[16] Woodward continued to produce wonderful work for another three decades, even winning the Pulitzer Prize in 1982 for editing *Mary Chesnut's Civil War*, but nothing that he did subsequently reoriented our understanding of a field as thoroughly as *Origins* and its early companions had done.[18] If for no other reason, *Origins* would be in our lives today because it is such an important part of the intellectual history of the field of Southern history and the story of America in the last half of the twentieth century.

Notes

1. That essay is the immediately preceding chapter in this volume.
2. C. Vann Woodward, *Origins of the New South, 1877-1913* (2nd ed., Baton Rouge, 1971).
3. C. Vann Woodward, *Thinking Back: The Perils of Writing History* (Baton Rouge, La., 1986), 67.
4. C. Vann Woodward, *Reunion and Reaction: The Compromise of 1877 and the End of Reconstruction* (Boston, 1951).
5. Allan Peskin, "Was There a Compromise of 1877?" *Journal of American History*, 60 (June 1973), 63-75.
6. Jonathan M. Wiener, *Social Origins of the New South: Alabama, 1860-1885* (Baton Rouge, La, 1978); James Tice Moore, "Redeemers Reconsidered: Change and Continuity in the Democratic South, 1870-1900," *Journal of Southern History*, 44 (August 1978), 357-78.
7. Woodward, *Thinking Back*, 64-65; Gavin Wright, *The Political Economy of the Cotton South: Households, Markets, and Wealth in the Nineteenth Century* (New York, 1978); David Carlton, *Mill and Town in South Carolina, 1880-1920* (Baton Rouge, La.,1982).
8. Leon Litwack, *Trouble in Mind: Black Southerners in the Age of Jim Crow* (New York, 1998); Joel Williamson, *The Crucible of Race: Black-White Relations in the American South Since Emancipation* (New York, 1984).
9. J. Morgan Kousser, *The Shaping of Southern Politics: Suffrage Restriction and the Establishment of the One-Party South, 1880-1910* (New Haven, Conn., 1974); Michael Perman, *Struggle for Mastery: Disfranchisement in the South, 1888-1908* (Chapel Hill, N.C., 2001).
10. Richard Hofstadter, *The Age of Reform: From Bryan to F.D.R.* (New York, 1955).
11. Lawrence Goodwyn, *Democratic Promise: The Populist Moment in America* (New York, 1976); Elizabeth Sanders, *Roots of Reform: Farmers, Workers, and the American State, 1877-1917* (Chicago, 1999). See also Steven Hahn, *The Roots of Southern Populism: Yeoman Farmers and the Transformation of the Georgia Upcountry, 1850-1890* (New York, 1983).
12. See especially James C. Cobb, *Industrialization and Southern Society, 1877-1984* (Lexington, Ky., 1984).
13. Glenda Elizabeth Gilmore, *Gender and Jim Crow: Women and the Politics of White Supremacy in North Carolina, 1896-1920* (Chapel Hill, N.C.,1996).
14. Edward L. Ayers, *The Promise of the New South: Life After Reconstruction* (New York, 1992).
15. Woodward, *Thinking Back*; John Herbert Roper, *C. Vann Woodward, Southerner* (Athens, Ga., 1997); and Roper, ed., *C. Vann Woodward: A Southern Historian and His Critics* (Athens, Ga., 1997); Howard N. Rabinowitz, *The First New South,*

1865-1920 (Arlington Heights, Ill., 1992); John B. Boles, *The South Through Time: A History of an American Region*. Vol. II, 2nd ed. (Upper Saddle River, N.J., 2003).

16.   Woodward, *Tom Watson, Agrarian Rebel* (New York, 1938); *The Strange Career of Jim Crow* (New York, 1955); *The Burden of southern History* (Baton Rouge, La., 1960).

4

The South as a Counterculture

All around us extraordinary crises threaten to intrude into the serenity of our daily lives, and we are aware as seldom before of the striking disjunction between the personal and the public realms. At this time, when the habits of mind formed by our national historical experiences with individualism, affluence, progressive growth and military victory seem to be interfering without ability to face up to the problems of racial justice, poverty, environmental despoliation and war, we should ask how our regional heritage speaks to our present needs. As the nation's largest and oldest counterculture, the South has much to teach us.

This, no doubt, seems a bizarre assertion to those familiar with the making of the contemporary counterculture. Much of the impetus for the cultural rebellion of youth lately has come from the assault of the civil rights movement on the South in the 1960s, so it would be a supreme irony if there were strong resemblance between the culture of the South and the culture created by young Americans seeking alternative values.

As analyzed sympathetically by Theodore Roszak in *The Making of a Counter Culture*, today's counterculture is at bottom a revolt against the dehumanizing effect of scientific and technological values, and against the bureaucratic society whose very efficiency depends upon desensitizing people to individual needs and differences. Artificial barriers that separate people, be they psychological, institutional, or social, say the current rebels, have to be torn down. In contrast to the ideal of material progress through rational analysis, the counterculture focuses on the quality of life and the need for individuals to have more power over the decisions that affect their lives.

Reprinted from *The American Scholar*, Volume 42, Number 2, Spring, 1973, pp. 283-293.
Copyright 1973, by the United Chapters of Phi Beta Kappa.

The revolt against authoritarianism in favor of the New Left's ideal of participatory democracy has become more generally a revolt against authority of any kind. Only personal experience can serve as the basis of belief, a precept that should be appreciated by Southern Protestants who trace their form of worship back to the frontier. As R. D. Laing, one of the prophets of the counterculture, expresses it, "We do not need theories so much as the experience that is the source of the theory."

The New Left itself began as a collection of young people with personal commitments but without a theory. Despite its polemical sloganeering and factional infighting over tactics in the late 1960s, it has been a movement in search of a theory, an ideological wasteland. Always, as with the civil rights movement, which it overlaps, members of the New Left were as interested in changing themselves, getting their heads on straight, as in changing the world around them. The unspecified nature of this search for self-liberation and personal autonomy is reflected in a vacuity of the expressions that have been generated from within the ranks of the disaffiliated youth. When one is "getting it together" or "getting with it" or "getting it on" or finding out "where it's at," even if "it's nowhere," one is never sure what "it" is. Like, wow, man, it's outasight, whatever it is, but *it* need not be specified because *it* is supposed to be perceived intuitively and not intellectively.

Whatever one thinks of the counterculture, one should not be too hard on its frequent resort to mindless slogans, such as "up against the wall" and "power to the people." The straight culture matches this tendency with commercial hucksterism and the adman mentality. Every time you wince at the call for "relevance," I hope you also shudder at the demand for "fiscal responsibility." When those who wish to "off the pigs" are confronted with the demand to "love it or leave it," wisdom will be found on neither side.

Similarly, one should take care not to judge either the counterculture or the straight culture by the perversions. Hypocrisy and self-delusion are the monopoly of neither. If adherents of the counterculture can be criticized for being so presentistic that they revel in instant gratification and hedonism, the credit card culture sports a hedonism of its own. The self-indulgence of the dude and his chick who talk of revolution amidst billows of Acapulco Gold and stereophonic sound is not different in kind from the self-indulgence that is rampant in our consumer society. To balance those who seek instant fulfillment on acid trips, there is the burgeoning human potential movement among the middle class. For every commune peopled with youth seeking a sense of community and purpose, there is a group therapy or sensitivity session in progress somewhere in suburbia. The team spirit promoted in corporate America is but a different variety of the solidarity sought by the young. The drug scene is matched by the cocktail hour.

Having made these equations, it is still possible to think of the counterculture as a different set of values and not just a different manifestation of the same malaise that is observable in the straight culture. In simplistic terms, it is a matter of the heart versus the head. There is widespread feeling that the life of reason has failed us because so many barbarities are perpetrated in its name and so many evils exist within its sight. The technocratic rationalism of the war in Vietnam is the thing that lends it a special horror.

Furthermore, so the argument goes, technocracy and bureaucracy stultify spontaneity and thus make individual authenticity impossible. In contrast to the innovative thinkers of the late nineteenth and early twentieth centuries, such as Sigmund Freud, who were interested in the nonrational in order to control it better, we are confronted with Norman O. Brown, who argues that civilization's discontents will remain unless currently repressed instinctual drives are released from control by the superego. At the risk of putting the matter even more simplistically, the counterculture is a protest against the commercialization of life.

What are we to make of all this from our special vantage point in the South? I begin with history, because I accept as truth what Jack Burden says in Robert Penn Warren's novel, *All The King's Men*: "If you could not accept the past and its burden there was no future, for without one there cannot be the other, and…if you could accept the past you might hope for the future, for only out of the past can you make the future."

The key to the Southern past is that Southerners are Americans who have taken on an additional identity through conflict with the North. The process differentiating the South from the American non-South in the early nineteenth century was based on divergent economic interests growing from differing labor systems, and depended in part upon the Southern context of a sparse, occupationally homogeneous population and the lack of an urban middle class. With that beginning, the Southern sense of separateness has been constructed on many layers of defensiveness, particularism, isolation, guilt, defeat, and the reactions to changes initiated from without: abolitionism, the Civil War, Reconstruction, poverty, depressions, industrialization and lately the civil rights movement. Through all this, white Southerners learned to see themselves as an oppressed minority with a giant sense of grievance, an identity they share with blacks, although for different reasons.

The counterattack of the Southern press against the hypocrisy and self-righteousness of the North during the Second Reconstruction is but another activation of this traditional defensive mentality. The same siege mentality can be seen subtly at work among historians and others who attribute the slow pace of modernization in the South to the region's colonial status and the imperial domination of Northern economic interests. Furthermore, the sense of persecution can be seen influencing the literature of the region. When Quentin Compson in *Absolom! Absolom!* comes to call on Rosa Coldfield before going off to Harvard, he is reminded, as he must have been a thousand time before, of the Yankee's persecution of the South. "So," says Rosa Coldfield, "I don't imagine you will ever come back here and settle down as a country lawyer in a little town like Jefferson since Northern people have already seen to it that there is little left in the South for a young man."

Nevertheless, Southerners are Americans, and in a real sense the need to be different was forced upon them by circumstances and by outsiders. The resulting approach-avoidance relationship of South to North explains why one finds in the South the coexistence of hyper-Americanism and cultural peculiarity.

The "approach" side of this curious psychological transaction can be seen best since the Civil War in the New South movement, beautifully dissected by Paul Gaston in *The New South Creed*, one of whose messages is that a conquered people frequently will imitate its conquerors. The chief tenet of the New South crusade is that industrialization is the way to secular salvation, and its optimistic dogma has from the first been that the South is destined to be the most prosperous place on earth, a new Eden. The bearers of these glad tidings were not only wise men out of the North, but local prophets as well, of whom Henry Grady was the most renowned in the nineteenth century. Today's champions of the New South tend to be the more institutional, hungry utilities and state industrial development officers, but the message is the same: The South is the land of milk and honey, or at least of water and electricity, and one can move into this land of low taxes and docile labor with little of the difficulty experienced by the children of Israel.

Southerners, when operating on the "avoidance" side of the American mirror, traditionally have had to define themselves in opposition to the presumed American norm, and in that sense at least, the South is a real counterculture. When the South was first created, the North was becoming the special carrier of Yankee commercial culture with its stress upon hard work, thrift and the cash basis of value. The mythical Southern planter, created in novels as an alternative to the emerging Yankee, was therefore a noneconomic man, the result of the South's need for a myth that would distinguish it from, and make it morally superior to, the North. The planter was not the uninhibited hero of whom Norman O. Brown would be proud, but he did have qualities that would recommend him to Charles Reich, whose recent book, *The Greening of America*, prophesied the collapse of the whole achievement ethic in America with the advent of Consciousness III.

The planters of the legend, explains William R. Taylor in *Cavaliers and Yankees*, were exemplars of noncompetitiveness. They were generous, loving, gentle, noble and true to their word. Rather than the instinctive nobility of the unspoiled savage, however, the planter had the benefits of a benign and salubrious country life and rigorous training in a civilized code. But it was not the code of the Yankee. The legendary planter was free of personal ambition, particularly of the material sort, and his natural impulses were disciplined, not by calculation of gain, but by his concern for family and racial traditions, by rigid standards of decorum and a complicated code of personal honor. That our fictive hero was also weak, improvident, indolent and ineffectual betrays a flaw of disbelief on the part of his creators and explains why (Oh, confounder of women's liberation) Scarlet O'Hara always ended up running Tara. Southern writers shared more than they realized of the mainstream cultural values of the nation.

Northern writers, conversely, played an important part in the creation of the plantation legend, but for reasons differing from those of their Southern brothers. Faced with severe social dislocations growing out of geographic mobility, industrialization, immigration and urbanization, some Northerners began to fear the erosion of the old republican style of life characterized by simplicity and prudence. In growing numbers during the decades before the Civil War, such men began to focus their discontent on the planter and the slave system upon which he depended, as the primary threat to the Puritan virtues upon which the republic was founded. At the same time, many other Northerners were becoming painfully aware that the helter-skelter process of social mobility in America could not monitor the conditions under which men competed, and thus could not guarantee the moral worth of the man who succeeded. The image of the Yankee as an acquisitive, grasping, uncultivated and amoral man was not acceptable to many sensitive Northerners. Some reacted by imputing to the Yankee transcending social virtue. They argued in effect that the ascetic, single-minded, materialistic and opportunistic Yankee benefited society by making a profit. Others, however, helped to create the planter of the Southern gentleman as the counterpoint to the Yankee. The Southern gentleman was made to possess all of the virtues that the Yankee lacked. He had honor and integrity, indifference to money questions and business, a decorous concern for the amenities of life and a high sense of social responsibility. In the age of democratic expansion, anxious men sought an antidemocratic Good Society and they found it in the mythical, static, Southern plantation.

Southern intellectuals responded obligingly by spending an enormous amount of energy romantically constructing Biblical or feudal or classical Greek alternative to the liberal capitalism of the nation at large. John C. Calhoun, to an extent, and George Fitzhugh, more fundamentally, attacked the dehumanization inherent in the wage slavery of free enterprise. According to Fitzhugh in his books, *Sociology For The South or The Failure Of Free Society* and *Cannibals All: or, Slaves Without Masters*, free competition was only legalized exploitation. It was merely freedom for the strong to oppress the weak. Anticipating Herbert Marcuse, one of the political philosophers of the New Left, Fitzhugh pointed out that not only was physical wretchedness the result of this war of all against all, but psychological wretchedness as well. For under capitalism one man's success was marked by another man's failure; fortunes shifted rapidly, and the result was that the human personality was marked by insecurity, anxiety and unhappiness. To complete his rejection of Jefferson, Fitzhugh advocated strong and positive action by the government to build up industries and cities in the South. Rejecting the doctrine of progress and the principle of equality, Fitzhugh held that only within the framework of absolute dependence and superiority could genuine reciprocal affection exist between human beings. A society seeking solution in fantasy could scarcely get further away from the American consensus.

After the Civil War, the mutual symbolic interaction of North and South continued under the new conditions. While the myth of the New South was being created in a great rush of popular fervor, the myth of the Old South was simultaneously being created, packaged and marketed in the North and the South. Reflecting this divided mind of the South, Joel Chandler Harris recorded his Uncle Remus stories at the same desk where he wrote for the *Atlanta Constitution* editorials infused with New South boosterism. Harris, George Washington Cable, Thomas Nelson Page, Mary Noailles Murfree and their fellow writers in the 1880s established the primacy of Southern themes in American letters. Archaic romance and local color stories appealed to Northern audiences facing the reality of rapid social change in their daily lives. Southern sensibilities called for pathos balanced with the theme of sectional reconciliation. Through it all ran an intense sense of place and awareness of the past-in-present that are trademarks of Southern literature. The stock Southern character, for Northern as well as Southern writers, was still the embodiment of noncommercial nobility, the counterpoint to the shrewd but crude robber baron who ruled the Gilded Age.

The Agrarians, a group of Southern intellectuals centered at Vanderbilt University in the 1920s and 1930s, did not perpetuate this cavalier myth, but they were nonetheless engaged in the old Southern sport of defining an alternative to the national consensus. As their manifesto, *I'll Take My Stand* put it in 1930, "All the articles bear in the same sense upon the book's title-subject: all tend to support a southern way of life against what may be called the American way; and all as much as agree that the best terms in which to represent the distinction are contained in the phrase, Agrarian versus Industrial." It was a frontal assault on the principles of Northern and modern civilization, a continuing comparison between the disordered present and the heroic past, which has always been the currency of groups disturbed by change.

The Agrarians, echoing George Fitzhugh, denied the virtue of machine-produced wealth and decried the brutalization of man and the philistinization of society that inevitably resulted from an industrial order. As humanists, they insisted that labor, the largest item in human life, should be enjoyed. This was impossible under industrialism. The art and culture they held most valuable was that which grew out of natural folkways of doing, living and thinking. All else was superficial. Present day devotees of the *Whole Earth Catalog,* organic gardening and the handicraft industry would find this pretty heavy stuff.

More abstractly, the Agrarians placed the relationship of man to nature close to the center of their philosophy. They believed that "there is possible no deep sense of beauty, human heroism of conduct, and no sublimity of religion, which is not informed by the humble sense of man's precarious position in the universe." In other words, "there is more in the land than there is in the man," as John Crowe Ransom put it, "Nature wears out man before man can wear out nature...It seems wiser to be moderate in our expectations of nature, and respectful; and out of so simple a thing as respect for the physical earth and its teeming life, comes a primary joy, which is an inexhaustible source of arts and religions and philosphies." The thing that differentiates these romantic conservatives most clearly from their descendants among today's youthful counterculturists is that the Agrarians linked community with continuity. They thought that "tradition is not simply a fact, but a fact that must be constantly defended." Nevertheless, paradoxical as it might seem, there is a large area of agreement between the culture of the South as understood by the Agrarians and the contemporary counterculture.

Like all paradoxes, the similarity between the culture of the South and the counterculture has its limitations. The world view of Southern Protestantism, which dominates the mind of the region, makes a virtue out of suffering in a way members of the counterculture would not understand or accept, even though the emphasis upon redemption through a personal conversion experience might find some resonance among young Americans seeking instant salvation along various secular and spiritual paths. Just as the counterculture is unthinkable in a country lacking the affluence provided by the work ethic in league with technocracy, Southern culture would not long survive apart from the rationalism whose hegemony it was created to challenge. The problems of human survival are not going to be solved by consulting the *I Ching* or Tarot cards.

Even so, at the present, when ten times more college students take courses in astrology than in astrophysics, when middle Americans, numbered by their lives as members of endless audiences, are in search of affective relationships, the South has much to offer. To an increasingly fragmented world the South offers an integrated view of life. There is no such thing as being "in fashion" now; styles in clothes and in most areas of life are too various and are multiplying too rapidly for a single standard to exist even for a short time. Contemporary art runs a gamut from the Wyeths to Helen Frankenthaler, and style has become a collective noun. Such currently popular writers as Donald Barthelme and Jerzy Kosinski render life into brilliant snippets of experience that coagulate without melding. Compare this to the vision of William Faulkner in which past, present and future are linked together; in which individuals don't merely rub up against each other in fleeting encounters but are enmeshed in each other's lives; in which individual lives over long periods of time are bound together by their connection to place. There is wholeness to life in the South, even in its harsh and ugly aspects, and this is a useful antidote to a world in which increasing individuality means increasing isolation.

The price of wholeness is finitude. Freedom and the power to act are circumscribed when one is tied to a community. Rather than something that a counterculture must construct in the future after all the restraints of organized society have been cast off, community for Southerners is a set of conditions and obligations to be fulfilled through courage and honor. Strangely enough, Southerners, both white and black, do not feel alienated from themselves even though they feel alienated from the national sources of economic and political power.

It may also seem strange to find illegal defiance of national authority coexisting so comfortably in the South with superpatriotism, but that is a consequence of the dual identity of Southerners, and grows out of their double history. As C. Vann Woodward points out in *The Burden of Southern History*, the South's experiences with defeat, poverty and guilt have set it apart from the nation. In contrast to the national belief that problems have solutions, Southerners harbor the countervailing suspicion that there are limits to human power.

There is a salutary humanistic lesson in discovering the vine of fate entangling Southern history. Whether that vine is wisteria or kudzu may vary according to ideological taste, but the message that there are areas of life not susceptible to rational control or bureaucratic manipulation strikes a resonant note. As a perceptive journalist observed of a group of irate town fathers in Mississippi who had just been struck by another federal court edict, "Of course, they are not really surprised because, being Southerners and therefore fatalistic, they live always half expecting disaster. "For those non-Southerners who lived through the 1960s it seems appropriate to sing "the good it seems they all die young," and although we may not have come to see the world as an unpredictable malevolent obstacle course on which, as in *Catch 22*, Nately's whore stalks us all, we do harbor suspicion that a thoroughgoing rationalism will never be able to control those unseen hostile forces.

Southern history forces us to be aware not only of complexity, but also of defeat and failure. It would be wrong to reject or oppose the improvement in social welfare that will come from the intrusion of the machine into the garden, but we should oppose the Icarian notion that change comes without costs, and that the South will be immune from history. Only through such a constant realization do we have a chance to industrialize and humanize at the same time, to walk the thin line between defeatism and morally obtuse boosterism.

In striving to live with our past without being oppressed by it, the proper stance is one of ambivalent judgment, an ironic distance between oneself and his history that energizes rather than immobilizes. The modern man facing his existential predicament might well be guided by the lesson contained in the following Hasidic legend recorded by Elie Wiesel in his book, *Souls on Fire:*

> One of the Just Men came to Sodom, determined to save its inhabitants from sin and punishment. Night and day he walked the streets and markets preaching against greed and theft, falsehood and indifference. In the beginning, people listened and smiled ironically. Then they stopped listening: he no longer even amused them. The killers went on killing, the wise kept silent, as if there were no Just Man in their midst.
>
> One day a child, moved by compassion for the unfortunate preacher, approached him with these words. "Poor stranger. You shout, you expend yourself body and soul; don't you see that it is hopeless?"
>
> "Yes, I see," answered the Just Man.
>
> "Then why do you go on?"
>
> "I'll tell you why. In the beginning I thought I could change man. Today, I know I cannot. If I still shout today, if I still scream, it is to prevent man from ultimately changing me."

5

The Clay County Origins of Mr. Justice Black: The Populist as Insider

An uncomplicated view of Hugo Black exists, a view that connects his role as a powerful dissenter on the Supreme Court, the champion of individual liberty and free speech, with his origins in the populist stronghold of Clay County, Alabama. According to this view, Black was a natural-born tort lawyer, a consistent defender of "the little man" against members of the social or economic elite and especially against concentrations of power and privilege.

Arriving as a complete outsider in Birmingham, Alabama, in 1907 to begin his legal career, Black received no invitation into an establishment firm, but began to scratch out a living as a personal injury attorney representing the working man and sympathizing with unions. From those humble beginnings, he became a reform-minded police court judge, anti-establishment solicitor (prosecutor) of Jefferson County, winner of a populist-style race for the United States Senate, staunch proponent of the New Deal and attacker of the malefactors of great wealth as a tough Senate investigator, and finally, Franklin Roosevelt's first appointee to the Supreme Court. As Supreme Court justice, Black fashioned an influential philosophy of the Constitution based on a Madisonian antipathy toward concentrations of power and on a fervent belief in individual freedom as clearly defined in various parts of the Bill of Rights, especially the first and fifth amendments.[1]

Assuming this neo-populist framework, the task of the biographer is fairly straightforward. The vignettes fall neatly into place with the exception of a few recalcitrant facts, and they can be explained as acts of political expediency—not laudable but certainly understandable in an aspiring politician in Alabama in the first third of the twentieth century.

This essay first appeared in the *Alabama Law Review* (Spring 1985) from University of Alabama Law School.

When Hugo Black joined the Ku Klux Klan in 1923, it was a major force in Alabama politics. The Klan was antiblack, anti-Catholic, anti-Jewish, and antiforeigner, and it used violence and intimidation to force wayward individuals of any description to conform to the code of personal morality of the white, Protestant, rural majority. The Klan was intolerant and extralegal and was the pathological form of the common white people's attempt to control the forces of change threatening their world. In addition, Hugo Black showed nativistic sympathies by favoring immigration restriction during his Senate campaign, exploited racial prejudice in defending Edwin R. Stephenson for killing a Catholic priest, suppressed, as solicitor, newspapers carrying illegal liquor ads, defended the handling of the Scottsboro Boys case with anti-Yankee rhetoric, and opposed the antilynching bill during his second term as senator.

On the other hand, even more numerous examples demonstrate Black's enlightened populism. For example, the case that established his legal practice in Birmingham was his successful recovery of damages on behalf of a black man who illegally had been kept at work in the mines beyond his prison term under the convict lease system. Many other instances of unusually fair treatment for blacks and poor whites under Hugo Black's regime as police court judge and county solicitor followed. Black's major legislative effort as a senator was the Black-Connery Bill, which would have provided for a thirty-hour week. Though never enacted, portions of the Black-Connery Bill found their way into the Fair Labor Standard Act of 1938.

Unless one make unusual demands for purity and enlightenment in the context of Alabama politics before, for example, the Voting Rights Act of 1965, Hugo Black's public career appears unproblematic; it is the story of the rise of an unusually talented and energetic proponent of "the common man." The biographer might want to grapple with the psychological problem posed by Black's personality: our foremost twentieth-century champion of individual liberty and free speech was himself a strict disciplinarian at home, domineering everywhere, and conventional in most matters of personal behavior.[2] Then again, this characterization would serve a good, general description of Black's idol, Thomas Jefferson.

Such were my assumptions on the only occasion that I was ever in Black's presence, a lengthy afternoon visit in 1964 arranged by my wife, Lucy Durr, the daughter of his first wife's sister. Having married Black's adoring niece, I also had absorbed the Durr family view of "Uncle Hugo," a view that combined unqualified admiration of the public man and love of the charming, devoted, and involved family man with a muted realism about Uncle Hugo's stubbornness, his strong-willed, competitive, and to some extent, stern personality.

I was still, on that occasion, a graduate student at Yale University at work on a study of Alabama in the Populist and Progressive era, but I had met and talked with several of Justice Black's former law clerks. Through their eyes, Justice Black appeared as an unusually hard-working justice and a demanding taskmaster, but he was also an exceedingly charming and thoughtful boss who took a deep personal interest in each of his clerks, just as he did with each member of his extensive family and hundreds of friends. Characteristically, they reported that Justice Black tolerated their arguing points of law with him, even encouraged it, but he never gave in to their point of view. They might notice that he subsequently would change his position on a topic about which they had been arguing, but he never would acknowledge that his clerks had caused him to change his mind.

All of these family perspectives were confirmed for me during that memorable afternoon of conversation in the comfortable upstairs study of his house in Alexandria. I was properly awestruck, so I remember few of the details of our conversation. I do recall making a mental note, in my worst graduate student style of one-upmanship, that Justice Black's view of Reconstruction was not up to date, nor did his ample shelves contain the most recent academic histories. Then, when cocktails were served, Justice Black made a point of explaining that his doctor had prescribed a drink before dinner; otherwise, as I knew, he never drank and had been a prohibitionist in state politics.

The only passage of discussion that afternoon that has stuck in my mind, because it was so striking then, arose as the three of us together watched the evening news on television. As was frequently the case then, a civil rights demonstration dominated the broadcast. Lucy's and my sympathies were clear and unqualified, so I was surprised when Justice Black turned and asked whether we had noticed the looks on the faces of the demonstrators, looks of hatred and fanaticism. An animated discussion followed about the motives of demonstrators and the dynamics of protest movements that, accurately or not, is the principal residue in my mind from that occasion.

As I recall that vivid moment, Justice Black was not expressing his view, developed in later civil rights cases, that officials have a right to impose reasonable limits on the public use of governmental buildings—a view that accommodates itself to the fundamentalist version of the First Amendment by drawing a sharp distinction between speech and action.[3] He was noticing, however, the authoritarian and anarchistic elements at work in the civil rights movement, elements that eventually led to the fragmentation of the movement. His observation upset me then because he detected a protofascist tint in a movement that I tended to see in Manichaean terms as the forces of light battling the forces of darkness. Clearly, his sense of public order had been disturbed by what he saw, and I went away to puzzle periodically about the apparent contradiction this revealed in his personality. How could the champion of the "little guy," the public servant whose principles stemmed from populist protest against the established order, have such a strong commitment to public order and express such clear reservations about the most prominent "little guys" on the current scene?

Had I been better informed about recent constitutional history, I would have recognized in Black's attitude on that day the nub of his running argument with Felix Frankfurter about judicial restraint in the face of legislative will. Black so much distrusted power that he distrusted it in the hands of the people as well as in the branches of government, or at least in his view, the Constitution prescribes certain fundamental freedoms that even the people cannot abridge through their democratic representatives. In a system of rules, the rules had to be applied fairly, and even the majority ought not to be able to alter certain basic rules or rights.

The more I have thought and read about Hugo Black over the subsequent years, the more I have found inadequate the uncomplicated view of him as a great man who merely worked out a different way of applying the Populist principles of his boyhood as he found himself in larger and larger public arenas. In a region that likes its prophets and rebels to have a bit more of the maverick in them, Hugo Black climbed to the top with the principles of an outsider and the behavior of an insider.

There is, I discover, a way to read his life that stresses the conforming side of his nature. To begin with, he was raised in modestly privileged circumstances in Ashland, the county seat of Clay County, Alabama. The Clay County of his boyhood was a hotbed of populism, to be sure, but his own family were not populists. They were too prosperous and too much a part of the social fabric of the town to have joined such a political rebellion. Populism in Alabama was for those who lived on the economic margin or whose ties to the social order had been loosened by geographic mobility, downward social mobility, or some other alienating force.[4]

Also of note, Jeffersonian ideals, expressed in rhetoric about the worth of the common man as opposed to men of power and special privilege, was political orthodoxy in Alabama. The historian cannot distinguish Populist newspapers from Democratic newspapers by the slogans on their mastheads or the rhetoric in their editorials. "Equal rights to all; special privilege to none" was a commonplace motto on both sides of the political divide. Hugo Black as a boy would have absorbed equalitarian principles and a reverence for Thomas Jefferson without having to feel like a rebel, a dissenter, a marginal man, or an outsider. On the contrary, as the bright and energetic son of the town's leading merchant, Hugo undoubtedly grew up in relatively comfortable surroundings with a secure sense of his place and his family's place in the upper reaches of local society. Given this background, he was a natural "insider."

Nothing he ever did was very far away from the mainstream. At the University of Alabama Law School, he was an officer in his small class of twenty-three students. When he went to the rough, industrial, frontier town of Birmingham to practice law, he started from scratch, but he soon came to the attention of an older, more established lawyer who maneuvered Black into position as police court judge. He made that system work efficiently, yet fairly, with a combination of toughness and compassion. He may have offended the sheriff and the police on occasion, but he accomplished what the legal establishment and the general public wanted him to accomplish. Furthermore, he joined every organization in sight and became a popular teacher in the Baptist Sunday School, not an unusual way to build a legal practice and a natural thing for a gregarious, unmarried young man to do.

Later, after winning election as Jefferson County solicitor, he repeated his reformist performance. He released petty offenders from jail and, thus, angered the officials who were the beneficiaries of the fee system, prosecuted people without regard to their social position or influence, and cleared the docket in a whirlwind thirty months in office.

After a patriotic stint in the army, Black returned to Birmingham and pursued his very successful and highly lucrative practice as a plaintiff's attorney. At the same time, he built his political base to run for the United States Senate through activities that included joining the Ku Klux Klan and lining up allies in every county of the state. While becoming known as the young "Bolshevik" attorney in Birmingham, Black lived on the fashionable southside, belonged to the country club, and courted and married Josephine Foster whose family was about as close as Alabama then could come to landed aristocracy, though the current generation had left the land and had moved to town. Both Josephine and her sister, Virginia, served terms as officers of the Junior League in Birmingham, a charitable organization that allowed young women of the most socially acceptable families, while displaying their social status, to do good works. Ironically, the Junior League helped awaken the political sensibilities of Josephine and Virginia by bringing them into contact with the grim realities of poverty and racial injustice. This well may have played a part in Senator Black's broadening notion of justice and fair play.

Black waged another populist-style campaign in 1926 to win a peculiar, five-sided race for the United States Senate over John H. Bankhead, Jr., of Jasper, a corporate lawyer and coal mine operator whose father had died in office in the United States Senate in 1920 and whose brother William Bankhead was already an influential member of the House of Representatives. Once in the Senate, Black tried to avoid prominence in the election campaign of 1928 that split the South, and he remained a Democratic Party loyalist. He gradually became an influential member of the Senate, his wife became the president of the Senate wives club, and he acted as a political ally of the Bankhead brothers.

Soon after the election of Franklin Roosevelt in 1932, Black emerged as a leading New Deal loyalist in the Senate and made a national reputation as an advocate of the thirty-hour work week and as an investigator of the ocean mail subsidy program, airmail contracts, and utility lobbyists. For such services, including his backing of the court-packing bill, President Roosevelt made Hugo Black his first nominee for appointment to the Supreme Court in August 1937.

On the Court, Hugo Black was also a loyalist; he developed and maintained a deep regard for the Court as an institution, so much so that he became privately critical of William O. Douglas' personal life because it threatened to bring discredit to the Court. Conversely, he was able to maintain warm personal friendships with colleagues on the Court with whom he frequently disagreed.[5] One might also note that his, and the Court's, greatest mistake was its rule that upheld the arbitrary internment of Japanese-Americans during World War II, an act that can be explained by the patriotic loyalties of Black and his colleagues on the Court.

Hugo Black also remained loyal to Alabama even through the period following the *Brown* decision when he widely and publicly was reviled at home and when some of the animosity toward Justice Black was taken out on Hugo Black, Jr., and his family, then living in Birmingham. Through those dark days when the justice could not visit the state with any pleasure, he continued to favor Alabamians for his clerkships and to stay in touch with family and friends at home.[6]

How then might we reconcile these two differing views of Hugo Black, the populist dissenter and champion of the ordinary individual against the power of entrenched economic interests, and Hugo Black, the institutional loyalist and patriot with an aversion to unseemly personal conduct and disorderly behavior? How could the same man be such a natural "insider" that he put institutional loyalty high on his list of values and became a superb organization politician, but be "outsider" enough that he allowed his Democratic sympathies to guide him throughout his career as a public servant, politician, and federal judge?

I believe the answer is to be found in Clay County, in his secure upbringing that made him a natural "insider," in the Jeffersonian social values that were the common coin of politics, and in the morality of personal responsibility that was the civic side of rural Protestantism.

Hugo Black, in one of his rare interviews in later years, remarked that most of his ideas came from the Old Testament.[7] I believe that was true. As the historian of ethics and behavior in the Old South has written about southerners of a slightly earlier period, "[t]hey had a sense of oneness with ancient values—both Old Testament and classical—concepts that still had pertinence in lives of hardship and inequality."[8] Black's remarkable self-education in the classics and in the history of the Revolutionary era merely confirmed the moral code that he had absorbed as a boy from his family and community, a code that owed as much to Old Testament concepts of duty as to Jeffersonian concepts of rights.

Whether one has in mind the laws or the prophets, the Old Testament is full of stories having to do with duty, with what an individual owes God and his fellow human beings. The thread that ties together the view of Black as an uncomplicated populist and the view of Black as an institutional loyalist is the strong sense of responsibility that Black had and thought everyone else also should have. He especially thought that people in positions of power should be punctilious in their observance of the rules. His devotion to this notion of fair play, rather than any personal identification with the oppressed classes, governed Black's strong sense of justice. He was much more concerned with the fair functioning of the system and with the proper execution of responsibilities than he was with transferring power to the working class.

For Hugo Black, liberty and responsibility were not separate values, but necessarily were linked as the defining dimension of his public philosophy. His public philosophy mixed Old Testament requirements and Jeffersonian ideals in a way that could have been accomplished only by a great man who came naturally by both sources of wisdom in his native Clay County, Alabama.

Notes

1. The author leaned heavily on V. Hamilton, *Hugo Black: The Alabama Years* (1972). The other standard biographical source is G. Dunne, *Hugo Black and the Judicial Revolution* (1977). For convenient sources of Black's opinions, see generally I. Dilliard, *One Man's Stand For Freedom: Mr. Justice Black and the Bill of Rights* (1963); Durr, "Hugo Black, Southerner," 10 *Am. U.L. Rev.* 27 (1961); Haigh, "Mr. Justice Black and the Written Constitution," 24 *ALA. L. Rev.* 15 (1971).

2. See *H. Black, My Father, a Remembrance* 92-93 (1975); G. Dunne, *supra* note 1, at 43; Durr, "Hugo L. Black: A Personal Appraisal," 6 *GA. L. Rev.* 1, 7-9 (1971).

3. "Justice Black and the Bill of Rights," 937, 943-45 (1977) (reprint of CBS News Special, Dec. 3, 1968). 9 Sw. U.L. Rev

4. *See* S. Hackney, *Populism To Progressivism In Alabama* 23-31 (1969).

5. Cooper, "Mr. Justice Hugo L. Black: Footnotes to a Great Case," 24 *ALA. L. Rev.* 1, 6 (1971). 247, 248, 249

6. *See generally* Meador, *Justice Black and his Law Clerks*, 15 ALA. L. Rev. 57 (1962).

7. *See* Note, "Justice Black and First Amendment 'Absolutes': A Public Interview," 37 *N.Y.U. L. Rev.* 549, 562 (1962).

8. B. Wyatt-Brown, *Southern Honor: Ethics and Behavior in the Old South* 25 (1982).

6

Little Rock and the Promise of America

Early in the twentieth century, in 1903, W.E.B. DuBuis predicted in his classic book, *The Souls of Black Folk*, that in the United States the problem of the twentieth century would be the problem of the color line. In 1944, in another classic study, *An American Dilemma*, Gunnar Myrdal noted that "America is continuously struggling for its soul," a struggle occasioned by the harsh gap between the reality of racial discrimination and the uplifting ideals of the "American Creed." Near the end of the century, in 1992, while block upon block in South Central Los Angeles smoldered both literally and figuratively, Rodney King spoke plaintively to the people of his city and beyond, "Hey people! Can't we all get along?"

Using these three data points alone, one is tempted to conclude simply that racism persists and that all the blood and ink spilled in the cause of racial justice and reconciliation has been spilled in vain. That conclusion would not only be wrong and would denigrate some remarkable achievements, but it would also mask a fundamental shift in the nature of the problem. Over the course of the twentieth century, glorious new chapters have been written in the story of America's advance toward the ideal of human equality that our founding documents envisioned. Nevertheless, racism persists, and it has not only become more complex as our population has become more diverse in recent years, it has also changed in a fundamental way since the Little Rock crisis of 1957.

The Little Rock crisis was one of those critical moments in our national life when nine brave teenagers, through the commonplace act of going back to school in September, forced the county to recognize that we were falling inexcusably short of the ideals set forth in our nation's Constitution and Declaration of Independence. Those

This address to a conference marking the fortieth anniversary of the Little Rock school integration crisis first appeared in Elizabeth Jacaway and Fred C. Williams (eds.), *Understanding the Little Rock Crisis* (Fayetville: The University of Arkansas Press. Copyright 1999 by Jacoway, et al.

nine heroes and heroines paid a high price for their acts of courage, and we have all benefited.

We have gathered here forty years later to try to understand that event, to assess the degree to which it constituted a step forward in the struggle for human equality, to wring some meaning from it that might bring us together as an increasingly diverse and progressively atomized society. Having just discussed this episode with my freshman seminar at Penn, I approach our task with a spirit chastened by the relentless power of history to change the meaning of the past and by the sobering accumulations of the intervening years. My students, you see, were born in 1979 and 1980. Their *parents* were too young to have been aware of the Little Rock crisis of 1957!

Moreover, after they had watched Henry Hampton's marvelous documentary *Eyes on the Prize*, my students were virtually speechless. They simply did not recognize the America in which the drama of 1957 Little Rock played out. They are not innocent of racism, nor of the subtleties of current discrimination, but they simply could not comprehend a society that practiced legal segregation, a society in which the raw ugliness of violent hatred was so near the surface, and one on which the federal government was so timid in the pursuit of justice. For them, mostly white and completely non-Southern, with ideological orientations ranging from polite liberalism to gracious conservatism, there is the unspoken assumption that African Americans are full participants in the same moral universe as all other Americans.

That is one measure of the impact of Little Rock. Recall that in 1942, 68 percent of white Americans supported racially segregated schools; by 1985 only 7 percent did. In 1944, 55 percent of whites nationally believed that whites should receive preference over blacks in job hiring; by 1972 only 3 percent supported that reasoning. At the level of principle, at least, African Americans are now full participants in the American mainstream. We owe that leap forward to Little Rock and to the civil rights movement it helped to ignite.

A great chasm separates us today from the society of the 1950s, largely because the turbulent sixties redirected the course of history and changed America in fundamental ways. The change is so complete that young people have trouble imagining a different America. In my thinking, the sixties began with the *Brown* decision, the Montgomery bus boycott, the Autherine Lucy case at the University of Alabama, and the integration of Little Rock Central High School.

No one doubts the primacy of the 1954 *Brown* decision in accelerating the pace of changes that had been moving toward racial equality since at least the New Deal. A case can also be made for the primary importance of the 1955-56 Montgomery bus boycott. Out of that experience emerged a new leader, Martin Luther King, Jr.; a new civil rights organization, the Southern Christian Leadership Conference; and a philosophy of protest, nonviolent direct action—all of which were to play important roles in the civil right movement over the next decade.

Nevertheless, the crisis at Central High provided something else, something especially compelling. In addition to a set of heroes, the Little Rock Nine and Daisy Bates, whose performance encouraged the mobilization of black communities though out the country, Little Rock provided, for all the world to see, a morality play whose meaning was unmistakable. When the Arkansas National Guard turned back the nine black teenagers, literally blocking the door that led to educational opportunity and preventing model young Americans from treading the primary avenue of self-improvement that Americans had come to recognize as a fundamental right, the public saw a dramatization of the evil of exclusion. Because the drama in Little Rock was about the exclusion of blacks from education and thus from full participation in the American Dream, it communicated what was to become the theme of the era in a particularly powerful and clear way. By humanizing Gunnar Myrdal's social science research and translating his elegant words into a form of spectacle—of political theater—Little Rock provided the theme, the images, and the powerful narrative that sped America along the road to full inclusion. The successes of the civil rights movement grew from the movement's emphasis on inclusion. When put into a human drama, it was hard for Americans to imagine why young African Americans should be denied access to the means of self- improvement. The promise of American life has always involved equal improvement. The promise of American life has always involved equal opportunity; one of the duties of American life has always been the obligation for self-improvement. The visual drama of the confrontation in Little Rock drove home the moral lesson throughout the country that excluding any American from this central dynamic was intolerable. Forced to confront the contradictions in their beliefs, white Americans actually changed their hearts as well as their minds.

As fundamentally important as was the dismantling of the legal structure of segregation and the shift of white attitudes nationally, the full realization of racial equality was not achieved in 1957 and has not been achieved yet. There is still a disturbing gap between principle and practice. Indeed, one of the most discouraging developments of the past twenty years is that a steady diet of distorted media images and sound bites about welfare queens and Willie Hortons, frequently manipulated for political advantage, has convinced the public that the problem of discrimination has been solved, so no government action is needed (in fact, would be counterproductive), and the natural processes of democracy and the market, if left unhindered to work their magic, will integrate whites and blacks in a natural and unforced manner.

Unfortunately, we know from opinion surveys that substantial majorities of white Americans believe that racial discrimination today is not a serious problem. They are aware that discrimination exists, but they believe that the incidence is minor and that it can be overcome easily by individual effort. We also know that significant majorities of African Americans perceive racial discrimination to be a constant and oppressive fact of their daily lives. In itself, this is a dangerous disparity, as if whites and blacks were not living in the same society or where not talking with each other. Consider the immediate reactions to the verdict in the O.J. Simpson criminal trial: 70 percent of whites thought it was jury nullification, while 70 percent of blacks thought the verdict was proper. When perceptions of the same event can be so different, what chance does society have to develop the level of social trust to make collective decisions about common problems?

More important, we know from carefully done studies that significant racial discrimination does exist in housing, jobs, education, banking, the criminal system, and the ordinary encounters of daily life. Yet whites do not perceive these continuing injustices, perhaps because they continue to harbor negative stereotypes of black Americans. This is the challenge of the current era.

In our media-drenched environment, how do we break through the noise of distorted messages to communicate a clear and compelling portrait of the gap that still exists between the principle and the practice of equality of opportunity? Even though it sounds completely inadequate, given the magnitude of the task at hand, talk helps. Talk may not be all we need, but the more we talk to each other across all the lines of difference that separate us, the harder it is to sustain those negative stereotypes that inhibit full understanding. That is one of my conclusions from the three-year project of the

National Endowment for the Humanities that has just been com-pleted. It was called "A National Conversation on American Plural-ism and Identity." It brought Americans together in face-to-face groups, by radio and television, and on the Internet, to talk and to listen to each other about what holds us together as a society in the midst of our increasing diversity, what values we share and need to share, and what it means to be Americans as we prepare to enter the twenty-first century.

From my persistent eavesdropping on the national conversation, I can confirm the impression that is broadly held among journalists and social critics that Americans are worried about the fragmenta-tion of society. They sense that we are drifting apart—into edge cit-ies and homogeneous suburbs and gated communities, sitting iso-lated in front of our television sets and computer terminals, into multicultural identity groups. Robert Bellah and his colleagues refer to this as a "crisis of civic membership."[1] Robert Putnam has started a "great debate" nationally about the depopulation of "civil soci-ety," that common space that is neither governmental nor privately personal where Americans historically have come together to pur-sue common interests and to solve common problems.[2]

The good news is that there is an enormous amount of goodwill among Americans. They are eager to work with others from groups different from their own to find solutions to social problems and to overcome barriers of suspicion. This is an important clue to a strat-egy for the needed crusade for reconciliation. Multicultural taskforces at the local level, brought together to study and to solve locally iden-tified problems, are a wonderful way to improve the community while building civic commitment and breaking down the barriers that separate groups.

One of my other discoveries in the NEH's National Conversation is that Americans actually share a lot of attitudes and beliefs without being fully aware of it. Most important, they overwhelmingly revere the Constitution and the Declaration of Independence. They are firmly committed to the political values that underlie our founding docu-ments, and especially to the simultaneous pursuit of human equality *and* individual liberty. Those two ideals sometimes pull in opposite directions, but Americans are committed to both.

Similarly, Americans are committed to a spacious sphere of life into which all come on a basis of complete equality, judged by the same standards, and expected to obey the same rules, a sphere of "just Americans" without any hyphenations or group modifiers. At the same time, they also want to be able to preserve the diversity of cultural heritages that serve to enrich our lives and connect us to our ancestral traditions. They respect diversity, but they also want this to be "one America, indivisible."

That determination to be a single nation was also the answer to the challenge put to the nation by the Little Rock Nine, Daisy Bates, and those who tried to accomplish that great step forward peacefully in accordance with the law of the land. The sympathies of an aroused nation, and the intervention of the federal government, affirmed that we were to be a single society, a unified nation.

Perhaps somewhere in our examination of the Little Rock experience we will identify the next step that our society must take toward the full realization of America's promise. Our guiding principle must be the observation of Martin Luther King Jr., "This is not a war between the white man and the Negro, but a conflict between justice and injustice."

The events in Little Rock forty years ago helped us realize that our fates as Americans are intertwined despite all our differences. We are bound together across barriers of time and boundaries of race, playing roles in a common story, sharing the shame of our shortcomings as well as the glory of our triumphs. The crisis in Little Rock is part of that grand narrative of expanding opportunity and equality, the progressively perfected inclusiveness of America.

Notes

1.   Robert Bellah, Richard Madsen, William M. Sullivan, Ann Swidler, and Steven N.Tipton, *Habits of the Heart: Individualism and Commitment in American Life,* updated edition with a new introduction (Berkeley: University of California Press, 1996), xi, xxx. The original edition was published in 1985.

2.   Robert Putnam, "Bowling Alone: America's Declining Social Capital," *Journal of Democracy* (July 1995): 65-75; and "The Strange Disappearance of Civic America," *American Prospect* (Winter 1996): 34-48. For an intelligent discussion and summary, see Scott Heller, "'Bowling Alone': A Harvard Professor Examines America's Dwindling Sense of Community," *Chronicle of Higher Education* (March 1, 1996). A scholarly exchange appeared in *American Prospect* (March/April 1996). See, for instance, Robert J. Samuelson, "'Bowling Alone' is Bunk," *Washington Post*, April 10, 1996; Richard Stengel, "Bowling Together," *Time*, July 22, 1996; and Nicholas Lemann, "Kicking in Groups," *Atlanta Monthly*, April 1996. Seymour Martin Lipset, "Malaise and Resiliency in America," *Journal of Democracy* (July 1995). For a different judgment, see Everett C.Ladd, "The Data Just Don't Show Erosion of America's 'Social Capital,'" *Public Perspective* (June/July 1996). A similar optimistic reading with regard to a single city is reported by the Pew Research Center for the People and The Press in *Trust and Citizen Engagement in Metropolitan Philadelphia: A Case Study* (April 1977).

7

C. Vann Woodward, 1908 – 1999: In Memoriam

C. Vann Woodward, Sterling Professor of History Emeritus at Yale University, the most widely admired historian of the United States in the twentieth century, died at his home in Hamden, Connecticut, on December 17, 1999. He was ninety-one years old.

Through superbly graceful prose and a gift for carefully qualified generalizations, Woodward recast the history of the American South in the period from Reconstruction to World War I, used the history of race relations in the South to instruct the nation on the possibility of overcoming racism, and accomplished the remarkable feat of shaping a distinctive understanding of American identity by illuminating the story of the region that served as its foil and counterpoint. His sensibility was essentially ironic, simultaneously aware of the likelihood of human failure but the moral imperative of effort.

Born and raised in Arkansas, the son of a teacher and school principal, Woodward came of age in the 1930s, which were beset with the Great Depression and the politics of scarcity. His sympathies were with the poor and the progressive, and his writings always reflected a keen awareness of contemporary political and cultural debate, yet his scholarship was rigorously grounded in evidence and free of tendentiousness. His first three books on the South were clearly addressed to questions of economic justice that dominated the decades of the 1930s and 1940s in the United States. His essays of the 1950s and 1960s were attempts to illuminate—one might say "expose"—with historical commentary the growing arrogance and complacency of the national mood. His work in the last three decades of his life was more eclectic and more in the nature of cultural criticism. It was also frequently philosophical, dealing with the nature and uses of history, or as he wryly put it, with "the influence of the

This appeared originally in the *Journal of Southern History*, LXVI, No. 2 (May 2000), 207-14.

present on the past." Woodward's writing reached a broad and important, though not popular, audience.

He produced masterful work in all the major modes of historical writing: biography (*Tom Watson, Agrarian Rebel* [1938]); monograph (*Reunion and Reaction* [1951]; and *The Strange Career of Jim Crow* [1955]); major synthesis (*Origins of the New South* [1951]; essays (*The Burden of Southern History* [1960], *American Counterpoint* [1971] *The Future of the Past* [1989], and *The Old World's New World* [1991]); scholarly editing (*Mary Chestnut's Civil War* [1981], with Elisabeth Muhlenfeld, *The Private Mary Chestnut* [1984], George Fitzhugh, *Cannibals All! Or, Slaves Without Masters* [1960], and Lewis H. Blair, *A Southern Prophecy* [1964]); general editing (*The Comparative Approach to American History* [1968] and the Oxford History of the United States series, still in progress); and intellectual autobiography (*Thinking Back: The Perils of Writing History* [1986]). It was a remarkable performance.

Woodward was recognized in almost every way a scholar can be recognized. He served as the president of all three of the relevant historical organizations: the Southern Historical Association (1951-1952); the Organization of American Historians (1968-1969); and the American Historical Association (1969-1970). He was also elected to membership in the American Academy of Arts and Letters and the American Philosophical Society. *Mary Chestnut's Civil War* won the Pulitzer Prize in 1982.

Woodward came to the practice of history late and reluctantly, thinking historians very pedestrian in comparison to the "renaissance" of southern literature that was then in full flower. He studied literature as an undergraduate at Henderson College in Arkansas and also at Emory University, where he transferred for his final two years. He continued to love literature and to read broadly all of his life, a practice that is evident in his own writing and in his friendships with Robert Penn Warren, Cleanth Brooks, and William Styron, among others.

He attempted graduate school in sociology at Columbia University in 1930-1931 for two dreadful days before switching to political science, which he found little better. Consequently, he spent much of his time in New York sampling the Harlem Renaissance and getting to know such figures as Langston Hughes. One can infer a lot about the young Woodward from the fact that wherever he was, he managed to get to know the most interesting people. Later, at Chapel

Hill, it was both President Frank Porter Graham and the "wrong crowd" of activist intellectuals who hung around the legendary Ab's Bookstore.

While teaching at Georgia Tech in 1929-1930 and 1931-1932 he made an important friendship with J. Saunders Redding and got involved in the defense of Angelo Herndon, an African American and a communist who was convicted and sent to jail for leading a demonstration against a reduction in relief funds for the unemployed. Woodward was soon unemployed as well, though he refused to believe that his radical activities had anything to do with his dismissal.

Still with vague literary ambitions, he began to work on a biography of Thomas E. Watson, a larger-than-life figure in Georgia politics, deceased only ten years earlier. While engaged in this effort, he met by chance Howard W. Odum who, with Rupert B. Vance, was the major intellectual magnet that made the University of North Carolina at Chapel Hill an exciting place in the 1930s. Odum was visiting his parents in Georgia, just a mile from the home to which Woodward's parents had moved at about the time Woodward transferred to Emory. Odum was impressed with the young writer and arranged a fellowship for him in history at Chapel Hill.

Woodward arrived in Chapel Hill in 1933-1934 with four chapters written and much of the research done on his biography of Watson. Four years later he submitted the typescript of his dissertation and sent a carbon copy to his publisher. It appeared in 1938 to warm review as *Tom Watson, Agrarian Rebel.* His advisor was Howard K. Beale, a leading historian who, with the more celebrated Charles Beard, championed economic interpretation. One can see the influence of Beale and Beard on Woodward's early work, though never in a heavy-handed way.

On the strength of that first book, Woodward was invited to do a volume in the LSU series of the history of the South. He taught successively at the University of Florida, University of Virginia, and Scripps College, all the while doing research on the post-Reconstruction South. That work was interrupted by World War II and service as an officer in the Navy. As soon as it was discovered that Woodward had published a book, he was assigned to naval intelligence and spent the war writing three books about naval battles, meant for quick distribution to the fleet for instruction and morale building. The third of those works was published as *The Battle for Leyte Gulf* (1947).

After the war, Woodward returned to the archives and also settled at The Johns Hopkins University in 1947, where he remained until moving to Yale in 1961.

The first fruits of his archival labors came in 1950 with the publication of *Reunion and Reaction,* an intricate detective story that revised the existing understanding of the end of Reconstruction in 1877. Conventionally, the "Compromise of 1877" was purely political. Southern politicians permitted the peaceful inauguration of Rutherford B. Hayes, a Republican, after the contested election of 1876, in exchange for withdrawal of the last Union troops from the defeated South (Florida, South Carolina, and Louisiana) and the appointment of a Democrat as postmaster general. Woodward discovered and traced an economic dimension of the maneuvering, involving Tom Scott of the Texas and Pacific Railroad who needed federal subsidies and could provide lucrative favors to politicians who might help enact the understandings among the various parties. Conspiracies are not always illusions, Woodward seems to say.

There is no doubt that this conspiracy existed, but whether it actually caused the deal to happen is a matter of inference and circumstantial evidence. Woodward's narrative is carefully qualified. As in so much of his work, ambiguity provides not only a touch of reality to the story but also gives it power and interest as well. Woodward's version of the "Compromise of 1877" is summarized in the first chapter of *Origins of the New South.*

This is a fascinating story of intrigue at the highest level, but it also introduces into the history of the post-Reconstruction South the theme of economic self-interest as a motivating force among the southern Redeemers, a radical departure from the conventional view of the time. In that view, the Redeemers were not only selfless regional patriots, but they were the antebellum ruling class rising from the rubble of war, this time to rebuild a South on the Northern industrial model, while preserving what was best about antebellum culture. The Civil War was not a disjunction, according to this view, it was just an unfortunate parenthesis, prolonged by the horrors of Reconstruction when the wrong sort (blacks, poor whites, and venturing Yankees) were in control. In short, the pre-Woodward celebratory history of the post-Reconstruction South was an apology for the existing regimes.

In *Origins of the New South*, Redemption was not restoration! In Woodward's telling, the story is not ennobling and uplifting. It is the story of the decay and decline of the aristocracy, the suffering and betrayal of the poor whites, and the rise and transformation of a middle class. It is not a happy story. The Redeemers are rapacious capitalists who mobilized the symbols of tradition in the service of change. The declining aristocracy are ineffectual and money hungry, and in the last analysis they subordinated the values of their political and social heritage in order to maintain control over the black population. The poor whites suffered from strange malignancies of racism and conspiracy-mindedness, and the rising middle class was timid and self-interested even in its reform movement.

There are no heroes in *Origins*, unless one considers such failed protest leaders as Tom Watson to be tragic heroes, or unless one views the dissidence of poor whites and blacks to be heroic even though futile. More important, Woodward successfully challenged the assumption of historical continuity across the Civil War and the notion that American history functions within a consensus that is free of class conflict.

Origins is a lament for paths not chosen, a continuing theme in Woodward's work. The colonial economy that resulted from Redeemer regimes was not good for the economic development or human welfare of the South. In particular, the failure of the Populist crusade, and the subsequent disfranchisement of blacks and poor whites, saddled the region with poverty, economic backwardness, and unresponsive political system, and the human misery that results from those things. Emblematically, Tom Watson, the leader of a class-based protest movement in the 1890s, soured into a race-baiting, anti-Semitic, and anti-Catholic demagogue in the first two decades of the new century.

The theme of "paths not taken" was pursued with regard to race relations in a series of lectures delivered in October 1954 at the University of Virginia that appeared in 1955 as *The Strange Career of Jim Crow.* It was by far the most popular, and most controversial book that Vann Woodward produced, going through five editions and three revisions. At the end of the march from Selma to Montgomery in 1965, with Woodward standing in the front row, Martin Luther King, Jr. called it "the Bible of the Civil Rights Movement."

What was strange about the "career" of Jim Crow, of course, was that it was of such recent origin. Segregation, far from being embedded in the folkways of the South, was a method of racial subordination that the white South stumbled toward fitfully after the end of

Reconstruction. This implies a period of flux in race relations that might have yielded a different outcome, had there been different leadership or different circumstances.

Instead, between roughly 1889 and 1908, the white South used the law to create a system of racial separation and subordination that was rigid, more-or-less uniform, and more-or-less universal. Some critics have questioned Woodward for implying that there was a golden age of race relations during Reconstruction and immediately after, and they have pointed to practices of racial segregation earlier than Woodward's thesis allowed.

Woodward frequently wrote more carefully than his readers read. He was not only aware that white animosity toward blacks survived the Civil War but also that local practices and customs frequently set blacks apart or even denied them the use of public facilities. Those practices, however, were not fixed; they varied from place to place and changed over time. With Jim Crow statutes, however, the system of racial subordination became fixed and virtually universal. The aspect that was useful in the 1950s and 1960s, of course, was that if the law was used to create segregation, it could be used to end segregation.

Almost every historian who writes about the South tries at some point to capture "the central theme" of Southern history. None has written more seductively than Woodward. Influenced by Reinhold Niebuhr, and alluding to his book, *The Irony of American History* [New York, 1952], Woodward sought the wellspring of the southern identity in "The Irony of Southern History," his presidential address before the Southern Historical Association in 1952, and in a series of other essays collected first in 1960 as *The Burden of Southern History*.

The burden of the title carries a triple meaning; it refers to the baleful presence of the past, to the obligation to apply to the present the moral lessons derived from the southern past, as well as to the "primary tendency" of the South's history. Southern history is a burden in the first sense because the faulty choices of those who went before have had devastating effects on contemporary southerners. In particular, the South's regional history differs from the major national myths of innocence, invincibility, and affluence because the South has experienced the guilt of slavery and subsequent systems of racial subordination, defeat in the Civil War, and wrenching poverty.

Writing well before the complacency of prosperity, the arrogance of power, and the sin of presumed innocence had led the United States into the horrors of the war in Vietnam, Woodward held up the possibility that the South's experiences might inform the national mood in such a way as to avoid the mistakes that were bound to flow from such hubris. Woodward himself recognized the irony of the fact that the South was in reality the seat of super-Americanism, the exaggerated version of the national mood that Woodward found so distressing.

Even though the country did not listen to him, thousands upon thousands of Southerners, black and white, who found themselves at odds with the dominant racial attitudes of their native region, derived solace and guidance from Woodward's point of view. To them, Woodward seemed to say, in word and deed, "follow your conscience. Not only is there a tradition of protest within the South that anchors your actions in history. But you also possess a dual identity that flows from the double history of being both a southerner and an American. That dual identity provides an ironic vantage point, where one can be a southerner without having to honor its retrograde myths."

Woodward's own life contained many contradictions. Among the most instructive of them stems from the fact that he was a politically engaged scholar whose work was a response to the dominant questions of the day. He committed himself very early in his political maturity to racial justice, and he never wavered from that commitment. He and John Hope Franklin desegregated the Southern Historical Association annual meeting in Knoxville in 1952. The following year, the two friends provided historical essays to Thurgood Marshall and Jack Green for their brief in the pathbreaking *Brown* desegregation case, decided in May 1954. *The Strange Career of Jim Crow* was a work of scholarship aimed directly at the most important domestic political issue of the twentieth century. He marched in Selma. He testified in the 1980s in favor of the extension of the Voting Rights Act of 1965, the major legislative outcome of the Selma protests. He even got involved in the 1990s in the protest against the proposal by the Disney Corporation to build a theme park near the Civil War battlefield at Manassas, Virginia.

Yet, he was also an intellectual leader who was eager to keep the academy free of politics and ideology. He opposed certain high-profile appointments at Yale that seemed to be based more upon

politics than scholarly merit, though it is also true that the most pub-
licized such incident came when he was in the depths of personal
despair and may therefore have been a less-generous act than was
typical. He was the chair of a famous ad hoc committee at Yale that
issued an eloquent report defending free speech and academic freedom from the demands of the radical left within the university. He
joined the National Association of Scholars, an organization devoted
to opposing the radicalization of universities.

The value that dissolves any apparent contradiction is intellectual
integrity. Woodward believed quietly but passionately in the wonderful myth that the search for truth is a cooperative enterprise. Thus,
one's critics are actually allies, fellow travelers on the road to discovery. *Thinking Back* displays this attitude in operation, as Woodward expresses his indebtedness to various critics who have changed
his understanding of a subject. He habitually replied gently, even
when he was not convinced by the criticism, and he readily changed
his position when he was shown to have been wrong or when a
better interpretation was offered.

The search for truth for Woodward was not only cooperative, it
was rooted in evidence. One of his differences with his good friend
David Potter was that he did not believe that there was a single "past
as it was." Just as the past impinges on the present, the present asks
different questions of the past and brings new understandings to it.
The critical thing is that the search for an understanding of the "truth"
be intellectually honest and grounded in verifiable fact.

Woodward supervised the dissertations of forty-two students. He
proudly had their books arranged together on a shelf in his sunroom.
Though he was never a spellbinding lecturer, he was a stimulating
seminar leader and an amazingly good critic of written work. In
him, his students had a model of intellectual integrity and scholarly
civility, and from him they received encouragement to pursue their
own ideas, even if that brought them into disagreement with him,
and even if it involved methodologies that he distrusted. He trained
no acolytes.

In contrast to the unrivaled success of his career, his personal life
was touched by tragedy. He lost his wife, Glenn, prematurely. Their
only son, Peter, died of cancer when he was a promising graduate
student at Princeton in political science. In his final years, he had
very few blood relatives in his life. On the other hand, his daughter-
in-law, Susan Woodward, a specialist on Eastern Europe, remained

close to him and his life was brightened by the companionship of Helen Reeve, a retired professor of Slavic languages and literature at Connecticut College. He kept up with numerous friends and former students.

Woodward never lost his subtle and self-deprecating wit. That, along with a keen intelligence that was always alive in the world, made him a delightful companion. His capacity for friendship was enormous.

He retired from active teaching in 1978, as early as possible, and spent an unusually productive retirement. Indeed, in this as in so much, he provided an admirable model. Up until his surgery in July 1999 to repair a heart valve, he was traveling on his own, working every day, taking daily walks, relaxing with a drink in the evening, and enjoying friends and loved ones. He never fully recovered from the surgery but died at home, sitting in his desk chair, amidst his books.

8

The Contradictory South

Not long after the reelection of President Clinton in 1996, while the sore losers were picking through the rubble trying to figure out how such a flawed character could win, and when the press was feasting on the story about the hazing of four women cadets who had rushed through the breach blasted in the walls of the Citadel by Shannon Faulkner the year before, a car going very fast passed me while I was driving on the Interstate from Washington, D.C., to Charlottesville, Virginia.[1] This would have been unremarkable had I not noticed as the other car pulled away from me that it sported two stickers on its rear bumper. One read, "Don't blame me, I voted Libertarian." The other simply announced its loyalty to "The Citadel."

My mind was occupied the rest of the way to Charlottesville with the puzzle of how the same person could harbor such contrasting sentiments, the one envisioning a life minimally constrained by externally imposed rules, and the other symbolizing submission to the most rigorous military discipline. There is, of course, the time-honored idea that some heroes must give up their individual freedom in order to protect the freedom enjoyed by the whole society. I suspect, however, that the occupant of this particular automobile was expressing a different and less altruistic notion. He was adopting an oppositional stance, embracing two unfashionable and contradictory loyalties in defiance of mainstream opinion, choosing an identity that set himself proudly apart from the herd-like majority.

It recalled to my mind an image of right-wing militias in camouflage uniforms holding training maneuvers in the woods while professing opposition to the authoritarian federal government, another instance of submitting to authority in order to oppose authority. The

This essay first appeared in Volume 7, Number 4 (Winter 2001) of *Southern Cultures*. It also appeared in Wilfred B. Moore (ed.) *Warm Ashes* (Columbia: University of South Carolina Press, 2003)

militias are attractive to a certain kind of person because membership allows one to be patriotically loyal and bravely subversive at
the same time. Such a mirror image identifies, like opposing strands
of DNA in the double helix, satisfying solutions to the tensions of
seemingly incompatible psychic needs.

In a similar fashion, Southerners, both black and white, maintain
an identity that is fully American, yet is at the same time a dissent from
America.[2] I mean to suggest here something more than the obvious fact
that Southerners are also Americans. Just as each of us has many different aspects to our separate identities, being a Southerner and an American presents no problem until the meanings of those two concepts clash.
They have been frequently at odds in the past, and their interaction
remains frequent and problematic. Over time, the result has been a double
or bipolar identity, analogous perhaps to the duality of a love-hate relationship, approach-avoidance mechanisms, or other deeply conflicted
orientations.

One of the traditional puzzles in the historiography of the South is
whether the South is quintessentially American with a few "peculiar
institutions" that it chose to defend, or whether it is a society whose
structure, values, and ideals of behavior are fundamentally different
from the rest of America. One could field a football team of distin-
guished historians on each side of this question.[3] The problem is made
more complex by the fact that the American identity itself is paradoxical. As historian Michael Kammen brilliantly argues, following an insight of psychologist Erik Erikson, the American identity is to be found
in the conversation between linked pairs of polar opposites, which
Kammen calls "biformitites," such as idealism and materialism, liberty
and equality, or individualism and community.[4] Those particular bipolar dialogues occur with a Southern accent as well. In addition, there is
the conversation, sometimes the argument, between an individual's
notion of being Southern and his idea of being American.

That the South is *both* American and alternative American is obvious at a superficial level.[5] Beyond that, how are the deeply conflicted ambivalences of being, say, a white Southerner/American
resolved or held in dynamic suspension by stances that can straddle
cultural contradictions? Black Southerners arrive at similar ambivalences by a path that mirrors that of their white counterparts. The
dual identity of Southerners grows out of the South's double history
(as both American and an exception to America), and it functions
comfortably within a culture shaped by biracialism and by a world

view whose model is Protestant Christianity's paradoxes of religious faith.

Consider this illustration. In a series of seductive essays in the 1950s and 1960s, C. Vann Woodward contrasted a Southern identity rooted in the un-American experiences of defeat, poverty, and guilt stemming from slavery and racial injustice with a national identity springing from a history of success, affluence, and innocence. Woodward here was engaging in the old literary tactic of using the South as a counterpoint to the North.[6] His subject was actually the complacent American mood of the postwar era and the dangerous arrogance flowing from the myths of American invincibility and purity of motive. The experience of the South, being much more akin to the human experience of the rest of the world, should serve as an antidote to the delusion that America was a chosen people, exempt from the consequences of hubris. Had America listened and learned from the "irony" of Southern history, we might have been spared the tragedy of the war in Vietnam.

As it happened, the nation did not listen. The United States was led by a Southern president, a Southern secretary of state, and a Southern commanding general into a war that could not be won, over matters that were not central to U.S. national interest. This foreign involvement generated increasingly strong opposition at home, leaving scars that have not yet fully healed. Ironically, the most hawkish section of the country was the South, the same South whose white inhabitants were simultaneously conducting a campaign of resistance to the federal government's authority in the area of civil rights and justice for African Americans, women, and members of other groups that suffered from discrimination. Here the South appeared in its dichotomous unity as the land of super patriotism and the locus of dissent.[7]

The South's multiple personality is obviously causally connected to its being both a part of the national story and at various times an impediment to that story. White Southerners and black Southerners share the double history of the region even though they may experience their relationship to it in ways that are inverse to each other. The self-consciousness of the South as a single, distinct region of the country with common interests was created during the debates over the Missouri Compromise in 1820, solidified in the defense of slavery against the abolitionist crusade, martyred in the Civil War and Reconstruction, extended by the rise and reign of Jim Crow, fed by perceptions of exploitation at the hand of Pittsburgh or Wall Street or Washington, and then reactivated by the struggle to resist the civil rights movement of the 1950s and 1960s. Through all of this it is clear that the identity was called into being originally by white apologists for slavery to oppose perceived threats to the "peculiar institution" from the outside. An oppositional mentality is one of the legacies of the white South's insistence for so long on some form of racial subordination as the defining feature of the social structure.

Conversely, being black in the hostile environment of the South has involved complex strategies of allegiance and opposition. Southern blacks and whites have been locked in a mutually modifying embrace, shaping and being shaped by each other and by a society whose core element is its biracial nature.[8] Whether or not biracialism finds institutional expression in slavery, in segregation, in some more fluid and complex public and private relationships, or in complete equality, there is still a twoness about living in the South. Yes, there are Cuban Americans in south Florida, Mexican Americans in south Texas, Cajuns in south Louisiana, Chinese in Mississippi, and triracial communities in Virginia and North Carolina, and a lot of fluidity and fuzziness at the margins of racial identities, but those and other complications don't yet challenge the formative power of biracialism in Southern culture. Marginality is interesting and important, but it should illuminate and not obscure what is going on at the center of the culture.

In addition to complications of racial identities, there also exists great variety along other dimensions of Southernness. Flatlanders differ from hillbillies, city folks from their country cousins, poor whites from gentry, and residents of the upper South from those who live in the Deep South. Despite the real variety, there is a shared identity, a sense of belonging to the same cultural tradition.

It has been widely accepted that the idea of the South—the social construction of the South as an American "other"—has been created and used by both Southerners and Northerners for political, ideological, and psychological purposes. There are so many possible intellective Souths, and so many different understandings of the American nation against which the South is being measured, that sociologist Larry J. Griffin warns us to ask with each invocation of the South, or of the American non-South, what the author is up to. What purpose is being served by this particular formulation of the Southern or the national identity?[9] That is a fair point. Since the socially constructed South must bear some relationship, however imperfect, to a verifiable, real-world South, we must also probe every evocation for its basis in the evidence.

To believe that there is a South and that it is based in some way on the formative power of biracialism is not to argue that all white Southerners believe in white supremacy or that every African American in the South is an incipient Nat Turner. It is to maintain, however, that every white or black Southerner must decide where he or she stands with regard to the tradition of black subordination. One can be a white liberal, a radical equalitarian, an unreconstructed segregationist, a leave-me-alone moderate, a black accommodationist, a black militant, or many other shades of racial consciousness. What one cannot be is nonracial. A large part of one's public identity as a white or a black Southerner is one's chosen relationship to the biracial nature of Southern society.

The South, of course, is not the only part of the United States with a regional consciousness and a special history. We all have stereotypical images of New England, Texas, the West, and California, for instance. Those images, however, are rooted in time past, in certain events (like the Battle of the Alamo), or particular periods (like the transplantation of town-meeting Protestantism to New England in the Colonial period, or the settling of the Great Plains in the nineteenth century by Europeans). The South, however, has a collective identity that was forged in conflict with the rest of the nation, was fixed by the grim realities of the Civil War, and has been renewed not only by continuing defensiveness but by the filtering of common developments and experiences through an awareness of regional difference.

During two periods of our relatively brief national history, the South has been the site of the central domestic political conflict: from the Missouri Compromise of 1820 through the Civil War and Reconstruction when the abolition of slavery dominated politics, and from the *Brown* decision in 1954 through the assassination of Martin Luther King, Jr. in 1968, when the civil rights movement was ignited in the South and then spread geographically to the rest of the country and demographically to other oppressed groups.

The realignment of American politics that came as a result of the Voting Rights Act of 1965 and as a reaction to the social justice and counter-cultural movements of the 1960s still defines the American political scene. A hugely disproportionate number of the leaders of both national parties now speak with Southern accents. Analysis of the controversial presidential election of 2000 confirms the fact that the South is now the most Republican region in the country. Even though the South is characterized by factors that predict Democratic votes (a large black population and lower levels of income and educational achievement), 55 percent of Southern voters supported the republican presidential nominee, who nonetheless failed to gain a majority of votes in the nation as a whole. Among Southern whites, 66 percent voted Republican.[10]

In short, unlike other regions, the South has played a major and continuing role in American politics, just as it has played a larger-than-life role in the American imagination. In the nonpolitical realm, the South has provided the nation with a scapegoat on some occasions, with compensatory "Song of the South" nostalgia that was meant to ease the tensions of industrialization and legitimize an unjust racial order, with dueling images of Tobacco Road versus Tara, with a convenient "Other" who could bear guilt or carry utopian dreams as the psychic needs of the nation required.[11]

As critic Louis Rubin points out, there are enduring and emblematic literary traits of Southern writers, whether black or white, male or female: "They are usually said to be a distinctive awareness of the past, a firm identification with a place, a preoccupation with one's membership in a community, a storytelling bent (as compared with a concern for problems), a strong sense of family and an unusually vivid consciousness of caste and class, especially involving race." Rubin also points out that though the factors that have commonly been used to explain Southern "difference" have disappeared, contemporary Southern writers continue to exhibit these hallmarks of southern literature.[12]

Despite its powerful and persistent presence, the South has been vanishing since Henry Grady began peddling his New South snake oil to the New England Society in New York in 1886; it is one of the longest and most theatrical exits on record. Just like Frederick Jackson Turner, who waxed eloquent in 1893 in his presidential address to the American Historical Association about the power of the frontier in shaping American culture just three years after the director of the census declared that the frontier no longer existed, observers seem to notice the formative power of one Southern characteristic or another only as they disappear.[13] Poverty, ignorance, rurality, isolation, ethnic homogeneity, and other supposed formative characteristics of the South have declined, but miraculously the South itself persists.

In his presidential address to the Southern Historical Association in November 1999, Jim Cobb wryly and wonderfully tweaked the noses of those who have pronounced premature epitaphs for Dixie over the preceding century and a quarter. He went on to argue that it is the North that has disappeared, dissolved by the discovery in the 1960s and 1970s that the stereotypical sins of the South were shared by the nation. That, of course, threatens the South because the South has existed as the foil of the North.[14] Left undecided is whether the South can exist without a utopian North and, if so, what will be the identity of the post-North South?

One should not infer from this, however, that just because the North has been exposed as harboring racial prejudice every bit as horrific as that found in the South, there is no real distinction between North and South. Anti-black feelings were rampant in the North during the antebellum period as well, but that did not make slavery less "peculiar" or less evil, nor did it prevent the Civil War. There is a fundamental difference between a society that contains racial prejudice and a society that is fundamentally shaped by biracial consciousness, whatever the current balance of power or mode of race relations happens to be. In the South, biracialism has guided residential patterns, business practices, civic activities, leisure pursuits, political arrangements, and almost every thread in the warp and woof of society. It is a substratum of the South's being.

Whatever the disappearance of the North portends, scholars and journalists are sure to continue their debate about whether the South still exists. One cannot deny that various indices of Southern distinctiveness continue to converge with the American non-South so that it is increasingly difficult to distinguish the region statistically.[15] Median family income in the South is closing the gap with the national average, and the responses to survey questions about time-honored litmus tests of Southernness are revealing less regional variation.

For instance, when a national sample of adults in 1993 was asked how often they ate an evening meal together as a family while they were growing up, there was no difference between Southern and non-Southern respondents. In the same survey, there was no significant regional difference in church going, or in saying grace before meals, or in entertaining a person of a different race in one's home, or in attitudes toward pornography, or in geographical closeness to relatives, or in preference for family over friends for leisure-time companions, or in attitudes toward military service as a qualification for elective office, or even in attending a stock car race.[16]

A 1992 poll asking whether the respondent favored racial integration, segregation, or something in-between found 55 percent of Southerners and 58 percent of non-Southerners in favor of integration and about 30 percent of both favoring something in-between. Only when the question was about interracial dating and marriage did Southerners show more resistance to racial mingling, and that difference is still present in a 1999 survey. On the other hand, a survey in 1996 found similar responses from Southerners and non-Southerners to a question about the desirability of hate-crime legislation, and similar percentages in 1999 claimed that the racial composition of their neighborhood made no difference to them. Could it be that it is finally time to play taps for the Southern mystique?

Don't blow that bugle yet! The South lives. The reason for the interminable disappearing act is that the South actually *is* constantly disappearing, only to be replaced by another South, also distinct but distinct in a different way. I think of this as the "molting South," always in the process of shedding a skin only to reveal another skin of original design covering the same beast.

Now, it is true that some of the persistent Southern identity is simply in the minds of Americans, North and South. For instance, in the same 1993 survey that found indistinguishable answers between Southerners and non-Southerners on questions about family behavior, there was this question as well: "In general, do you think Southerners are more loyal to family or less loyal to family than people in other areas of the country?" A majority of both Southerners (68 percent) and non-Southerners (56) percent thought that Southerners were more loyal to family. Similarly, although there are now only small differences between South and non-South in churchgoing, large majorities, of both Southerners (72 percent) and non-Southerners (68 percent) in a 1993 poll thought Southerners were more religious. Perceptions of Southern distinctiveness persist, even though it is difficult to capture some of those differences in objective measurement.

A representative sample of adults was asked in the summer of 1999 whether or not their community was in the South. Of the eleven ex-Confederate states, only Texas (84 percent) and Virginia (82 percent) fell below the 90 percent level in respondents who believed their community was in the South. The suburbs of Washington and the Texas borderland are nibbling at the edges of Southern self-consciousness. Kentucky (79 percent) and Oklahoma (69 percent) remained as pretenders to Southernness, while other states that are sometimes referred to as "Southern" contained only minorities who thought of themselves as living in the South: West Virginia (45 percent), Maryland (40 percent), Missouri (23 percent), Delaware (14 percent), and the District of Columbia (7 percent). The idea of the South is alive in the minds of ordinary people.

It is also true that the South still exists in the world of measurable differences and real human action. The South maintains its position as the most violent and the least schooled part of the country. It is still the poorest and the most enamored of gun ownership and capital punishment.[17]

The Federal Center for Disease Control and Prevention recently issued a report warning the public that obesity is a public health problem in the United States. The nation is fat and getting fatter, and the South is leading the way. Traditional Southern cooking might be part of the problem, the report concluded, but the "more likely reason for the greater increase below the Mason-Dixon line is the lack of exercise. Southerners are less likely to hike, ride a bike, walk, or join a health club than people in the rest of the nation."[18]

Another recent government study reported that the state of literacy in the country was not good, and it found the South particularly illiterate. Of the eleven ex-Confederate states, only Virginia had fewer than 20 percent of its population in Level One literacy (the worst category). All the rest had 21 percent or more of the population in Level One literacy. Of the non-Southern states, only California, New Jersey, New York and the District of Columbia, all places with large numbers of immigrants and high levels of poverty, had 21 percent or more of their populations in Level One literacy.

So, the sedentary South and the ignorant South join the cavalier South, the lazy South, the militant South, the violent South, the demagogic South, the benighted South, the sunny South, and other exotic Souths on the shelf of national curiosity. Tempting as it is to define the South as that part of the United States that is fat, dumb, poor, and violent, to do so would be to confuse transitory symptoms with lasting identity.[19]

The recent controversy about the confederate flag flying over the South Carolina state capitol reminds us that the siege mentally, while no longer claiming a majority of white South Carolinians, is still aggressively alive. That was confirmed for me not long ago when I spotted a Confederate-flag bumper sticker on a shabby pickup truck in Alabama whose text read, "If At First You Don't Secede."

Tony Horwitz found enough Confederates in the attic to give one pause. For a certain part of the Southern white population, within the vibrant subculture of Civil War reenactments and the popular market for Civil War symbols and memorabilia, he detects a continuing sense of grievance and of loss. Theirs is a struggle to save a world that is slipping away, in which big government serves as the proxy for an unseen enemy and the Confederate battle flag is the talisman against modernity.[20]

Even though pollsters have difficulty asking questions about racial attitudes that differentiate Southerners from non-Southerners, practicing politicians in the South know that racial attitudes still motivate a significant portion of the electorate in a way that is not true outside the South. Cynthia McKinney, a black woman running for reelection in 1998 to the U.S. House of Representatives in a redrawn white-majority district, played the "reverse race card," appealing to the progressive whites in the neighborhoods around Emory University to demonstrate to the country that Atlanta was beyond racism. It worked. She was reelected.

Obversely, Zell Miller, former Democratic governor of Georgia, told an audience of Southern historians in November 1999 that it had been a political mistake for him to try to purge the Confederate symbol from the Georgia state flag in 1992-94, not because he had changed his mind about the morality of the situation but because he had rebalanced the political equation. It was an error, he concluded, to have expended huge amounts of political time, energy, and credibility on an issue that was merely symbolic but about which a majority of the white voters felt very strongly. It distracted attention from "real" issues.[21]

Miller's advice for white Democrats was to avoid the buzz-saw symbolic issues and talk about things government can do to improve the lives of ordinary folks, black as well as white. The formula for success is well known to white Democrats, he said. They must get 90 percent of the black vote and 40 percent of the white vote. The implication is clear. Any issue tinged by race will chase enough white voters away to allow the Republicans to win. Sure enough, the Georgia legislature's recent removal of the battle flag motif from the state flag is proving to be unpopular. Symbolism has a reality of its own.

Another way to think of the continuing presence of race in the thinking of the Southern electorate is to ask the question "Why is the South the most Republican section of the country in presidential elections?" It is certainly not because the South contains a disproportionate share of the educational and economic elite who find Republican policies appealing, though it is true that a certain kind of elite is involved. When the federal government first began to cater to the needs of people at the local level during the New Deal, it was intruding into the province of local elites in the South. The economic order was threatened as well as the racial order. The flip-flop to the Solid Republican South after 1968 occurred because the Republican Party came to represent resistance to the federal government's threat to the intertwined racial and economic arrangement of Southern society. The Republican Party also represented a brand of self-reliance that struck a responsive chord in a region not far removed from its agricultural past and thoroughly imbued with its Protestant present.

Just as W. J. Cash made much of the simultaneous presence of hedonism and pietism in the ordinary Southerner, the GOP is harvesting the fruit of a hybrid formed by the union of traditionalism and free-market capitalism. Traditionalism honors the authority of patriarchy, community, and older ways of doing things. The market is devoted to material values, innovation, and self-interested individualism. Nothing is more corrosive of tradition than the market. It is a case of the contradictory loyalties of the Republican Party matching the contradictory psychic needs of the white South.

While it is difficult to disentangle cause and effect, it is still clear that the transformation of the Democratic South into the Republican South had something to do with the fact that the Religious Right is centered in the South. The Religious Right is dedicated to resisting the drift of our culture toward secularism, hedonism, and materialism. One of the large ironies of the present day is that the Religious Right has identified the Democratic Party as the sponsor of modernist cultural values. Thus it has allied itself with the Republican Party, the party that claims to be both the preserver of family values and the champion of free-market capitalism and technological progress, the very forces that inevitably undermine those values that the Religious Right seeks to preserve. It is not unusual to find that a major trend in American culture has generated its own negation; it *is* unusual to find both the thesis and the antithesis in the same political party. As modern life has gotten more self-serving and pleasure seeking, the opposition to it has become more Southern, even though Southerners participate enthusiastically in the materialism of modernity. This is another instance of double consciousness.

The function of religion in Southern life, however, is probably more subtle and more powerful than is suggested by the political activism of the black church or of Pat Robertson's Christian Coalition. Protestant Christianity provides the unconscious culture model for Southerners who seek to understand the world and their place in it. The overwhelming Protestantism of the South subtly shapes a culture in which people find their identities in the paradoxes of theological assumptions, in the conversation between conflicting culture commandments, in the dialogue between the opposing poles of the dichotomous choices they face in daily living.

Christians know Jesus as both Lord and servant. They simultaneously view Him as both human and divine. These are overarching contradictions that believers embrace with no trouble. The example of Christ embodies the Christian paradox that you cannot save your life except by giving it away, and it is held aloft as the ideal for emulation by Christians. The Christian promise that "the last shall be first" helps shape a worldview that is constructed on important contradictions.

The evangelical dilemma, then is that people are all absolutely responsible for their sins and for the state of their souls, but they are powerless without the help of God to save themselves. Men and women are at the same time radically independent and abjectly dependent. The evangelical Christian struggles to understand and to live a godly, righteous, and sober life, yet salvation comes through grace, a free gift from God.

The secular analogy is that we are all expected by society to be responsible for our own well-being, but we are incapable by ourselves of sustaining ourselves. We are not only social animals, but we live in a modern society composed of intricate arrangements that make each of us dependent in some way on each other—for a job, for police protection, for a market in which to sell the products of our hands and head, for a government that will educate our neighbors so they can also contribute to society rather than prey on us, for laws that will guarantee our ownership of all kinds of property against the rapacious designs of predatory individuals and organizations, for the provision of common goods like clean air and water, roads and bridges.

The resulting tension between individualism and organization is a central theme of American history, a running argument between Henry David Thoreau and John D. Rockefeller, or perhaps between Clint Eastwood and Bill Gates. It occurs in the South with a regional flavor, refracted by the biracialism that has shaped Southern identity, and identity that is to be found in the cultural exchange between black and white, and between "just American" and "Southern American." Just as Christians embrace the dilemmas of faith, Southerners accept the paradoxes of their Southern identity.

The South is full of exemplary Americans and of alternative Americans at the same time. The American identity is multifaceted, and it changes over time, but whatever it is at any one time, the South is both American and its opposite, both endorser and critic. In short, Southerners, both back and white, live with paradox.

To be Southern is to have a public identity formed in a biracial world, a biracial world in which the interplay between blacks and whites has left each group profoundly influenced by the other, a biracial world that has created a hybrid culture shared by both groups. To be Southern is to be formed by a religious culture of contradictions, contradictions that are resolved by transcendent belief. To be Southern is also to be created in the conversation between the American identity and dissenting critiques of the American identity. To be Southern, either black or white, is to be profoundly contradictory.

Notes

1. Catherine S. Manegold, *In Glory's Shadow: Shannon Faulkner, the Citadel and a Changing America* (New York: Alfred A. Knopf, 2000).
2. For an interesting rendering of the "Oppositional South" theme, see Larry Griffin, "Why Was the South a Problem?" in *The South as an American Problem*, ed. Larry J. Griffin and Don H. Doyle, (Athens: University of Georgia Press, 1995), 10-32.
3. See, for instance, Carl N. Degler, *Place Over Time: The Continuity of Southern Distinctiveness* (Baton Rouge: Louisiana State University Press, 1977), 2-7, and Charles Grier Sellers Jr., ed., *The Southerner as American* (Durham: University of North Carolina Press, 1960; E.P. Dutton and Co., 1966).
4. Michael Kammen, *People of Paradox: An Inquiry Concerning the Origins of American Civilization* (Ithaca, NY: Cornell University Press, 1972, 1990).

5. See David L. Carlton, "How American is the American South?" in *The South as an American Problem*, ed. Griffin and Doyle, 33-56. Carlton's explanation from economic history is only a partial solution because it does not account for the contemporary doubleness of Southern identity.

6. C. Vann Woodward, *The Burden of Southern History*, revised and enlarged edition (Baton Rouge: Louisiana State University Press, 1960, 1968), and C. Vann Woodward, *American Counterpoint: Slavery and Racism in the North-South dialogue* (Boston: Little, Brown and Company, 1971).

7. See Randall Wood, "Dixie's Dove: J. William Fulbright, the Vietnam War, and the American South," *Journal of Southern History,* 60 (1994): 533-552.

8. For an interesting exploration of Southern blacks' sense of rootedness or community, see James C. Cobb, "Searching for Southernness: Community and Identity in the Contemporary South," in *Redefining Southern Culture: Mind and Identity in the Modern South* (Athens: University of Georgia Press, 1999), 125-149.

9. Larry J Griffin, "Southern Distinctiveness, Yet Again or why American Still Needs the South," *Southern Cultures,* 6 (2000):47-72.

10. For exit poll results, see the *New York Times*, 12 November 2000. Nationwide, 90 percent of blacks voted Democratic, as did 79 percent of Jews, while 63 percent of white Protestants and only 47 percent of Catholics voted Republican.

11. The classic statement of a mythic South created to counterbalance certain motifs of national character is William R. Taylor, *Cavalier and Yankee: The Old South and American National Character* (New York: Doubleday Anchor, 1961), 183. For a more recent examination of the same general theme, see Carl Degler's presidential address to the Southern historical Association in 1987, "Thesis, Antithesis, Synthesis: The South, the North, and the Nation, "*Journal of Southern History*, 53 (1987): 3-18.

12. Louis Rubin, "Changing , Enduring, Forever Still the South," in *The Prevailing South: Life and Politics in a Changing Culture*, ed. Dudley Clendinen (Longstreet Press, Inc., 1988), 226.

13. John Boles, ed., *Dixie Dateline: A Journalistic Portrait of the Contemporary South* (Rice University Studies, 1983). See especially Boles's introduction.

14. James C. Cobb, "An Epitaph for the North: Reflections on the Politics of Regional and National Identity at the Millennium," *Journal of Southern History,* 66(2000: 3-24, and George B. Tindall's "Beyond the Mainstreet: The Ethnic Southerners," in *The Ethnic Southerners* (Baton Rouge: Louisiana State University Press, 1976), 1-21. The first full treatment of Southern whites as an ethnic group is to be found in Lewis Killian's *White Southerners* (New York: Random House, 1970). Some superficial confirmation of this interesting observation is provided by the National Collegiate Athletic Association. The four regions into which the men's national basketball championship tournament is divided are: South, East, West and Mid-West. There is no North. In the women's tournament, conforming to Cobb's prediction, there is not only no North but no South either, just East and West and their "Mid" twins.

15. See Benjamin Schwarz, "The Idea of the South", *Atlantic Monthly*, December 1997, 117-126. My favorite empirical tracing of the existence of the South is John Shelton Reed's *The Enduring South* (Durham: University of North Carolina Press, 1974). See also John Egerton, *The Americanization of Dixie: The Southernization of America* (New York: Harpers Magazine Press, 1974); Peter Applebome, *Dixie Rising* (New York: Harcourt, Brace/Harvest Books, 1996); and Edwin M. Yoder, "Thoughts on the Dixiefication of Dixie," in *Dateline Dixie*, ed, Boles, 159-166.

16.   All survey results cited here are from the Southern Focus Poll conducted by Howard Odum Institute for Research in Social Science at the University of North Carolina at Chapel Hill, available on the web at www.irss.unc.edu/data-archive/Pollsearch.html.

17.   See Andrew K. Frank, "The End of the South?" in *Routledge Historical Atlas of the American South* (Routledge, 1999), 129-131

18.   *New York Times*, 27 October 1999.

19.   *The State of Literacy in America*, a publication of the National Institute for Literacy available online at http://www,nifl.gov/reders/reder.htm.

20.   Tony Horwitz, *Confederates in the Attic: Dispatches from the Unfinished Civil War* (New York: Pantheon Books, 1998).

21.   Richard Hyatt, *Zell: The Governor Who Gave Georgia Hope* (Mercer University Press, 1997), chapter 17.

9

Identity Politics, Southern Style

"There has been much talk about the politics of identity," writes Henry Louis Gates, Jr., "a politics that has a collective identity at its core. One is to assert oneself in the political arena as a woman, a homosexual, a Jew, a person of color . . . . The politics of identity starts with the assertion of a collective allegiance. It says: This is who we are, make room for us, accommodate our special needs, confer recognition upon what is distinctive about us. It is about the priority of difference, and while it is not, by itself, undesirable, it is— by itself—dangerously inadequate."[1]

Jean Elshtain has written compellingly of democracy as the working out of self-limiting freedom and of the current impediments to a healthy deliberative democracy. Among her worries is the rise of identity politics. She writes:

> Rather than negotiating the complexity of public and private identities, those who adopt this view disdain and displace any distinction between the citizen and whatever else a person may be—male or female, heterosexual or homosexual, black or white. One seeks full public recognition as a person with a handicap or a particular sexual orientation, or membership in an ethnic or racial group, and exhausts one's public concerns. Marks of difference, once they gain public recognition in this form, translate all too easily into group triumphalism as the story grows that the public world is a world of many I's who form a we only with others exactly like themselves. No recognition of commonality is forthcoming. We are stuck in what the philosopher calls a world of "incommensurability," a world in which we literally cannot understand one another.[2]

With conservatives gleefully shouting encouragement from the Amen Corner, the sorts of intellectuals formerly known as "liberals" squirm uncomfortably in the grasp of their identity-group allies from the sixties. Arthur Schlesinger, Jr., who is not a right-wing fanatic, has worried at length about the threat of tribalism.[3] Todd Gitlin, a veteran of sixties activism and a sympathetic critic of the tattered, postmodern remnants of the American Left, argues tellingly that

---

This essay first appeared in Anthony Dunbar (ed.) *Where We Stand: Voices of Southern Dissent* and is reprinted with permission by New South Books, Montgomery, Alabama.

multiculturalism in general, and identity politics in particular, inhibits and weakens the Left by precluding any notion or vocabulary of the common good.[4] One could easily multiply such examples. All decent Americans apparently abhor identity politics.

"Identity politics" is a subcategory of multiculturalism, and both of those terms have diverse meanings. In some usages, identity politics refers to any social transaction in which a person's group identity plays a part—and that is just about all social transactions. "The personal is political," ran the slogan from the women's movement in the sixties. "Accused of politicizing everything," Todd Gitlin writes, "identity politics responds that politics is already everywhere; that interests dress up as truth but are only interests; that power is already everywhere and the only question is who is going to have it."[5]

Here, however, I wish to focus more narrowly on the role of cultural identity groups in electoral politics. Further, I wish to grapple with an apparent contradiction. As David Hollinger noted in *Postethnic America*, "the United States is endowed with a *non*ethnic ideology of the nation;" yet "it is possessed by a predominantly *ethnic* history."[6] Similarly, George Frederickson observed in his presidential address to the Organization of American Historians in 1998, "Group membership may be produced by shared historical experiences and social status and not by genes or cultural essences, but ethnoracial identity provides a locus from which most Americans view the world and is a major determinant of whom they vote for, hire or promote, associate with, and welcome as neighbors."[7]

We excoriate identity politics in theory, but we embrace it in practice. In the real world, politicians and pundits, consultants and analysts, Right as well as Left, practice their crafts in terms of identity groups. For instance, we were told frequently during the 2002 midterm elections that the Democratic strategy was to produce as large a turnout as possible among black Americans, while the Republican strategy was to excite their base, especially the religious right. A glance at the exit poll results confirms that the professionals knew what they were talking about, and that the Republicans did a superior job.

Exit polls from the presidential election of 2000 make the same point in a more reliable way because turnout was higher. The reader will recall that the election was extremely close. Al Gore, the Democratic candidate, won the popular vote, but George W. Bush, the Republican candidate, carried the Supreme Court. For present purposes, the interesting thing is that the close vote was not evenly

distributed across all social groups. The South, black and white together, was the most Republican section of the country (55 percent).
Whites who described themselves as members of the "religious right"
gave 80 percent of their vote to Bush, while African Americans were
90 percent in favor of Gore. Jews nationally cast Democratic ballots
at a rate of 79 percent, as did Hispanic voters at the level of 62
percent, while Southern whites were 65 percent for the Republican
candidate.

There was also a huge gender gap in the 2000 election. Bush
attracted 60 percent of the male vote. While women in the aggregate
were very evenly divided, those who pursued careers outside the
home were decidedly in Gore's camp, while those who worked as
homemakers were for Bush. This is "family values" at work in the
polling place.

If one is tempted to conclude that the South is so heavily Republican because it is characterized by features that predict Republican
votes throughout the country, such as Protestant Christianity or rural
residence, one must also come to terms with the fact that the South
has disproportionate numbers of people at lower levels of education
and income, which are powerful predictors nationally of Democratic
votes. It is impossible not to conclude that Southern voters are being
moved by factors that are peculiar to the region. It is also prompts us
to think of white Southerners as an identity group, just like African
Americans.

Identity group politics is traditional in the United States. Historians of nineteenth century America have understood for some time
that identity group solidarity explained much more electoral behavior than other quantifiable variables. Industrial labor was frequently
organized in ethnic federations, and the New York City ethnically
balanced ticket is a running joke in political circles.

One of my favorite cartoons from the 1960s is by Jules Feiffer. It
contains eight panels, each one a drawing of LBJ's head. The President is speaking:

First, the Negroes revolted.
Then the Puerto Ricans revolted.
Then the youth revolted.
Then the intellectuals revolted.
In order to preserve law and order, I have had to put them all in jail.
But punitive measures are *not enough*. These troubled times cry out for new answers to
   unsolved *old* problems.

> To seek out the *causes* of anarchy and propose a *cure* I have this
> day appointed a *fact finding commission.*
> To this commission I am appointing
> 1 Democrat
> 1 Republican
> 1 Young Person
> 1 Old Person
> 1 Intellectual
> 1 Anti-intellectual
> 1 Negro
> 1 Bigot
> Come Let Us Reason Together.

When Bill Clinton in the 1992 presidential campaign deliberately
criticized Sister Souljah for her defense of "gangster rap" lyrics that
seemed to condone the murder of white policemen by black youth,
he was practicing a kind of identity politics. He was distancing himself from the white-fright stereotype of the black community; he
was repositioning his party in the minds of suburban whites who
viewed the Democratic Party as the sponsor of racial and ethnic minorities, and the promoter of countercultural values. When George
W. Bush speaks to a crowd in south Texas or Florida in Spanish, he
is practicing identity politics; his subtext is that the Republican Party
is not hostile to the aspirations of the Hispanic community. When
Pat Buchanan exhorted a Mississippi audience in the 1996 primary
campaign not to let "them" take America away from "us," the divide
among identity groups was clear.

Is this disjunction between what we do and what we profess merely
hypocrisy? The question is interestingly complex. In his comparative study of race in the United States, South Africa, and Brazil, Anthony Marx notes that almost everyone in Brazil notices that poverty increases as skin color darkens. Yet, no one, not even poor
blacks, attributes the poverty to racism. Marx's explanation is that
Brazil differs from the United States and South Africa in that the
state (the government) never acted to construct or define race as a
legal category. When the state codifies racial identity, he argues, it
perpetuates racial categories as significant social realities that facili-
tate discrimination against the group that is being marginalized. Ironically, the resulting racial solidarity is also useful to the oppressed
group when it mobilizes to liberate itself from racial oppression.[8]

This certainly fits the American case. Much of the meaning of being African American has been in the process of legal construction and constant revision since the seventeenth century. It has been constantly contested, of course, and it has changed dramatically over time, but the identity is rooted in the law and in a conflictual relationship with the Euro-American majority. The national Republican Party in the late nineteenth century gave Southern whites their way over race relations in order to knit the white nation back together after the Civil War and Reconstruction. The exclusion of blacks was the mechanism for the fusion of whites.

The race-baiting used against white racial liberals in the South was a way of suppressing dissent, and it had the added benefit of reinforcing the Southern white identity. Just as patriotism can be invoked to silence those critics who seem to oppose the nation when it is acting as the nation, race baiting worked in the South because the white Southern identity was originally and fundamentally a racial construction. This helps to explain the weakness of white liberals. They were marginalized at home, and they were also vulnerable to pressures from the cosmopolitan North where they desperately wanted acceptance and support. They were cosmopolitans living in a parochial culture.

There was some important white support for the civil rights movement when it assumed the guise of a mass movement in the 1950s and 1960s, but the Second Reconstruction was most importantly a mobilization of black communities and black institutions to abolish the legally defined disabilities of race. Those black institutions and the black consciousness of African-American communities had been made necessary by the legal strictures of segregation. Small wonder that African Americans see identity politics as a natural extension of interest-group politics.

Euro-Americans outside the South see things differently. Perhaps this is because, since the advent of "Black Power" in 1966, and the onset of the "ethnic chic" revival of the 1970s, identities of difference have for the first time in the twentieth century been asserted from below. Before the 1960s, despite the existence of theories of pluralism and myths of equalitarian assimilation—melting pot and mosaic—the single model available in the public arena for new Americans or excluded Americans was Anglo-dominance. It held that if you look and act and speak like old-stock Euro-Americans, you can blend in and be accepted. The strangle hold of Anglo-dominance was broken by the social justice movements of the 1960s. The new racial and ethnic equalitarian orthodoxy was represented in the Civil Rights Act of 1964, the Voting Rights Act of 1965, and the Immigration Act of 1965. The new dispensation blossomed in an increase in individual possibilities, a multiplication of legitimate models in almost every area of life. Consensus came to seem repressive. Aside from the familiar irony of teenage conformity to non-conforming modes of dress and behavior, standards of any kind became somewhat suspect.

We are still trying to find some accommodation to the sixties, some way of adjusting our ways of living and thinking to the new social realities, or some way to turn back the tide of change. The current "culture wars" are largely symbolic battles about the multicultural national identity that has its roots in the sixties. Reacting to the failure of the Senate to convict President Clinton, and distraught about the remarkably robust levels of public approval of the impeached President, Paul Weyrich, head of the Free Congress Foundation and hard-right moral crusader, announced to his constituents that the conservatives had "probably lost the culture war."[9] As welcome as that result would be, the ultimate outcome is actually not at all clear. It is clear, however, that there is widespread worry among the public about social fragmentation, the growing social, physical, economic, and cultural separation of Americans from each other. That worry is exacerbated by identity politics.

It is easy to recognize why black Southerners might view identity politics as a natural mode of promoting self-interest; the attitude of Southern whites takes a little thought. It is undoubtedly somehow linked to the cultural filter through which Southern whites view reality. If, as George Tindall invited us to do twenty-five years ago, we think of Southern whites as an ethnic group,[10] then the question becomes, "Why does the Southern white ethnic identity exert such a hold on its members? Why is Southern whiteness "unmeltable?"

Southern white identity was created out of conflict with the North. It was a social construction invented to fashion a consciousness of commonality among whites living in a slave society and therefore affected by the anti-slavery movement. Common African ancestry existed before "race" was "constructed" in the seventeenth century as a category that would permit slavery. Similarly, Southern whites shared the fact that they lived in a slave society before the abolitionist movement (whatever time you pick for the origins of that movement at a significant level), but it was that movement that created a consciousness of commonality because it was perceived by whites as a threat. Thus was invented a mythological people whose mission was to protect a besieged social order. This reading is true whether you think of slavery simply as an economic system or as a way of ordering a biracial society.

We know the history of this new identity group. Secession, defeat, Reconstruction experienced as revolutionary tyranny, the creation of the myth of the Lost Cause as a counterweight to New South apostasy, reconciliation with the white North at the expense of black Southerners, the creation of the Solid South in response to the threat of Populist political insurgency, the disfranchisement of blacks and the creation of a social order based upon racial segregation at the turn of the twentieth century, continuing white poverty that was interpreted as more oppression at the hands of the industrialized North, the rise to covert national power of the political leaders of the white Southern identity group between 1938 and 1968 in coalition with non-Southern Republicans, the undermining of that "system" by the Civil Rights Movement and the Voting Rights Act of 1965, and then the flight of Southern whites to the suburbs and to the GOP. The white South has been the most significant locus of dissent in America. Paradoxically, the South has been intolerant of internal dissent. Though there is a tradition of dissent within the white South— anti-secession, white Republicanism, Populism, racial liberalism, labor unionism, civil rights sympathizers, even the rumor of a communist here and there—the region has been as heterodoxically starved as it has been economically poor by comparison with the rest of America, making Southern white dissenters even more heroic than they otherwise would be.[11]

There is an explanation for that. The comparative scarcity of white dissenters in the nineteenth-century South may derive from the simpler social structure of a dispersed agricultural society. That society contained fewer non-geographical nooks and crannies where dissenters could achieve some insulation from a disapproving social order. It was a more homogeneous society with fewer elements of conflicting interests, and therefore fewer groups with the functional freedom to develop discordant beliefs.

Add to this the thought that American individualism in its nineteenth-century incubator justified itself in terms of the welfare of the whole community. Greedy, self-centered, atomistic, solipsistic individualism was not the American ideal. As Robert Wiebe has put it, "Free individuals formed democratic communities; democratic communities sustained free individuals."[12] This explains why Alexis de Tocqueville observed both rampant American individualism *and* an energetic associational life, and why Frederick Jackson Turner saw the frontier as both the birthplace of American individualism *and* of a barn-raising, corn-shucking cooperative ethos.

As David Potter long ago pointed out, the nature of individualism changed as the conditions of society shifted from the nineteenth to the twentieth centuries. In the nineteenth century, self-reliant individualism was in vogue because society needed people who could take care of themselves as they pushed their way across the continent or built an industrial economy. As the specialized roles of urban, industrialized life replaced self-sufficient farmers and independent craftsmen in the twentieth century, and as society needed independent action less and independent thinking more, individualism began to mean intellectual nonconformity or dissent. The sin of the nonconforming individualist, of course, is that he undermines the ability of the community to protect its values and self-image against the criticism or assault of outsiders. The community cannot tolerate that, especially a community like the white South that sees itself as besieged by alien forces.[13]

The South lived in the nineteenth century more thoroughly and longer than did the non-South. The result is the persistence of the sort of self-reliant individualism that acts to protect the community from nonconformity. Add to that the notion that the Southern white identity is the product of a series of perceived threats, and one can understand why confrontations with the "cultural other" will revivify the sense of crisis and reinforce parochial conformity. Parochial white Southerners experience a loss of liberty when the freedom of their group is threatened, whether the threat comes from the Civil Rights Movement, the counterculture, the federal government, or some phantasmagoric combination of the three.

If Dan Carter is right, as I think he is, about George Wallace being the precursor to the Republican ascendancy in Washington (the New Republicans), the meaning of the South in a curious sense has become the meaning of America. Or, at least, that is what is at issue in the present political battles. We should not miss the irony of the unintended consequences of black enfranchisement by the Voting

Rights Act of 1965. In 1972, the South was solid once more, but it was not Democratic.

Many have noticed the remarkable prominence of Southern political leaders recently. During President Clinton's second term, the president, vice president, speaker of the house and majority leader of the Senate were all from the South. When Newt Gingrich of Georgia self-destructed, he was replaced briefly by Robert Livingston of Louisiana, who was quickly discovered to have the same problem of not living according to family values. Then, the Republicans were apparently reluctant to have as the picture of their party the next two most senior possibilities, Phil Gramm and Tom DeLay, both Texans, and both, like Gingrich, carpetbaggers and fugitives from the academy. Dennis Hastert breaks the Southern hold on national leadership, unless you are among those who believe that he is the mouthpiece of Tom DeLay, the Republican majority leader.

When Senator Trent Lott in December 2002 heaped praise upon retiring Senator Strom Thurmond, and ventured the opinion that the nation would have been better off if Thurmond and the Dixiecrats had won in 1948, he was allowed to twist gently in the politically correct breeze before being eased out of the way so Senator Bill Frist of Tennessee could take his place as majority leader.

Thurmond's own place in the pantheon of Lost Cause heroes was put in jeopardy when, after his death in 2002, his daughter from a relationship between the young Strom and the even younger black maid in the Thurmond household, came forward in public for the first time. It wasn't that this sort of thing had never happened before, it was simply the monumental hypocrisy of it all. The prominence of Florida in the 2000 election, and of so many Southern politicians among the leaders of both parties, is not necessarily evidence of the natural superiority of Southern politicians.[14] It undoubtedly says a lot about the importance of the South to the electoral strategies of both parties. It is a battleground region.

Meanwhile, back in the Clinton administration, six of the thirteen house managers of the impeachment trial were white Southern men, and they were an extremely visible six. In contrast, their initial five-person witness list of people from the enemy camp "looked like America" (Monica Lewinsky, Sidney Blumenthal, Betty Currie, Vernon Jordan, and John Podesta)—two Jews, two blacks, two women, and one Greek/Italian hybrid. This tableau dramatizes Dan Carter's thesis that George Corley Wallace was the founding father of the New Republican Majority; he led the Southern white ethnic revolt against the federal government and against the party of big government because those two entities had been sponsors of the civil rights movement and of various other "out groups," opposition to which helped to define the Southern white identity.[15] Southern white ethnic animosities happened to coincide with the animosities of the stalwart core of the New Republicans: the cultural conservatives and the religious right.

Now, the reason identity politics arouses such suspicion is that it confounds the American belief in the liberty of self-definition. We are told by our culture that we can construct ourselves, and reconstruct ourselves. We can choose our own values and even our own identities. Even if we recognize ontological difficulties with this notion, and even if we believe that race is a "social construction," it is not for the most part an individual option, despite the clear lesson of Thurmond's biracial family. Identity politics is thus at war with a central feature of the American identity. Ironically, of course, it has been the denial of access to this self-determining, self-choosing realm of society that has caused some Americans to resort to identity politics in the first place.

If this is a fair abstract of a version of Southern political history and of the Southern white identity, several interesting implications leap out. First, of course, Southern whites have been playing identity-group politics since the abolitionists first raised their voices, and they have been particularly active in recent years. That blacks and other minority groups were coming under fire for practicing just the sort of identity group politics that has been traditional in the South is fundamentally unfair.

Second, surveying regional history since the Missouri Compromise in 1820, we must conclude that while the content or meaning of racial categories frequently changes, the categories themselves persist. They persist and they continue to shape, though not determine, the history of the region and its people.

Third, cultural identity is stronger as a political force than is economic self-interest. A long line of Southern liberals and sympathetic observers has operated on the assumption that the South could not be redeemed until race was somehow taken out of politics. That "somehow" was generally thought to be by a politics of economic self-interest that would bring together blacks and whites in a biracial coalition of the poor.[16] That was the road not taken in the Populist revolt of the 1890s or in the New Deal. In this tradition, Bob Dylan sang in 1963 about the murder of Medgar Evers:

> A South politician preaches to the poor white man,
> "You got more than the blacks, don't complain.
> You're better than them, you been born with white skin," they
> explain.
> And the Negro's name
> Is used it is plain
> For the politician's gain
> As he rises to fame
> And the poor white remains
> On the caboose of the train
> But it ain't him to blame
> He's only a pawn in their game.

As admirable as this liberal tradition was, it turned out that economic change stimulated racial change rather than the other way around. The Southern economy was industrialized and urbanized by the forces set loose by the mobilization for World War II. A prosperous South in the 1950s was thus more open to the black liberation movement, which in turn stimulated the intervention of the federal government.

One of the most interesting questions about Southern history is why neither the liberal reform movement nor New South capitalism was ever effective enough to bring about fundamental change from within the region. Change came from the outside—the very thing that the Southern white identity group always feared and always expected. Why that was so involves a long and complex discussion, which is not appropriate here, but it has to do with the white South practicing identity politics, and especially local elites using race-baiting to protect their short-term interests. It also features the presence of abundant rewards for racial scapegoating, along with the absence of wholesome alternatives to lives of limited economic opportunity.

The lesson here is that if we want a politics free of racial and ethnic identity groups, we must do two things. We must produce a society in which such group identities are irrelevant for anything being contested through politics. That means a society that provides equal opportunity in the fullest sense to all its members, a society that protects the full citizenship rights and civil liberties of everyone. This must continue to be the goal of Southern liberals and the passionate commitment of everyone who loves freedom and believes in democracy.

We also need an American identity capacious enough to include all Americans, an identity that contains a large sphere in which we all meet as equals and as individuals with the same rights and responsibilities, bound together by a common allegiance to the core values of our revitalized democracy, and by its common though perhaps contested history. At the same time, this common arena must welcome our diverse identities of descent as being legitimately American, and allow them to persist, to borrow from and lend to each other, without imposing disadvantages on any of their members.

The answer to the question of why the Southern white identity is "unmeltable" is that it has been periodically reactivated, awakened from its wary nap by changes that are perceived as threatening by whites who themselves feel alienated, marginal, and at risk. Progressive politics thus must propose public policies and community-building initiatives that benefit working Americans of whatever racial or ethnic group, that help people acquire the capacity to help themselves, that tie individuals into the wider society and let them feel at home in the global economy. For far too long has the South followed the catastrophic economic strategy of low taxes, low public investment, low wages, and low value-added enterprises. We must test every public policy by its ability to contribute to a wholesome long-term future in an interdependent world. Above all, we must oppose the politics of division, and support the politics of inclusion.

Distressingly significant numbers of Southern whites will continue to spend their energies in keeping other people down until their identities become more complex, more entangled with the kudzu of the heterogeneous world, more implicated in the American identity's embrace of the universal values in what Gunnar Myrdal called the "American Creed."

We should be able to be both Southern *and* American, just as black and white Southerners should see in each other an "other" who completes a whole. Blacks and whites in the South have been shaping each other's identity for almost four hundred years. It is impossible to think of either member of this pair without the other, and they each exist in tension with the national identity. Our national identity has ample room for both.

Notes

1.   Henry Louis Gates, *New York Times*, March 27, 1994. Also see "Goodbye, Columbus? Notes on the Culture of Criticism," *American Literary History*, 3 (1991), pp. 711-727; and "The Meaning of America," *New Yorker*, April 19, 1993, pp. 113-117. Gates is the Director of the W.E.B. DuBois Center at Harvard University.

2.   Jean Bethke Elshtain, *Democracy On Trial* (New York: Basic Books, 1995), 66. Elshtain is the Laura Spelman Rockefeller Professor of Social and Political Ethics at the University of Chicago.

3.   Schlesinger, *The Disuniting of America: Reflections on a Multicultural Society* (New York: W. W. Norton and Company, 1992).

4.   Todd Gitlin, *The Twilight of Common dreams: Why America is Wracked by Culture Wars* (New York: Metropolitan Books of Henry Holt and Company, 1995), especially 129-139, and 200-202.

5.   Gitlin, *The Twilight of Common Dreams*, 151.

6.   Hollinger, *Postethnic America: Beyond Multiculturalism* (New York: Basic Books, 1995), 19.

7.   Frederickson, "America's Diversity in Comparative Perspective," *The Journal of American History* (December 1998), 859.

8.   Anthony W. Marx, *Making Race and Nation: A Comparison of South Africa, The United States, and Brazil* (Cambridge: Cambridge University Press, 1998).

9.   *New York Times*, February 21, 1999.

10.   George Brown Tindall, "Beyond the Mainstream: The Ethnic Southerners," *The Ethnic Southerners* (Baton Rouge: Louisiana State University Press, 1976), 1-21.

11.   See, for instance, Anthony P. Dunbar, *Against The Grain: Southern Radicals and Prophets, 1929-1959* (Charlottesville: University Press of Virginia, 1981), and John Egerton, *Speak Now Against the Day: The Generation Before the Civil Rights Movement in the South* (New York: Alfred A. Knopf, 1994).

12.   Robert Wiebe, *Self-Rule: A Cultural History of American Democracy* (Chicago: The University of Chicago Press, 1995), 40.

13.   David Potter, "American Individualism in the Twentieth Century," in Gordon Mills, ed., *Innocence and Power: Individualism in Twentieth Century America* (Austin: University of Texas Press, 1965).

14.   For that argument, see David Leon Chandler, *The Natural Superiority of Southern Politicians: A Revisionist History* (New York: Doubleday and Company, Inc., 1977).

15.   Dan T. Carter, *The Politics of Rage: George Wallace, the Origins of the New Conservatism, and the Transformation of American Politics* (New York: Simon and Schuster, 1995), 466-468.

16.   V. O. Key, Jr., *Southern Politics in State and Nation* (New York: Alfred A. Knopf, 1949). One might also cite C. Vann Woodward's masterful study, *Origins of the New South* (Baton Rouge: Louisiana State University Press, 1951), and more recently John Egerton, *Speak Now Against the Day*.

10

Shades of Freedom in America

Like other Americans, my understandings of the world have been challenged by the events of September 11, 2001. On that fateful day, after I had absorbed the stark horror of the event, and noted with pride the amazing responses of Americans both far and near, and pondered the sort of fanaticism that employs terrorism, I began to wonder why al-Qaeda had chosen those particular targets. The two planes that crashed into the towers of the World Trade Center flew right by the Statue of Liberty. The plane that struck the Pentagon might as easily have hit the Capitol or the White House. We do not know the target assigned to the fourth plane that went down in Pennsylvania, beyond the surmise that it was headed for Washington, D.C.

It seems clear that the targets were carefully chosen for symbolic purposes. The World Trade Center and the Pentagon represented America's economic and military power. Conspicuously not chosen were symbols of freedom or democracy—not the Statue of Liberty, not the Liberty Bell, not Independence Hall, nor the home of Congress, nor the house of our elected president. I found myself thinking, "They have got us wrong." Well, if the meaning of America is not simply wealth and power, what is it? Who are we as a people, and how can we defend that core identity against terrorists and our more insidious enemies: sloth, greed, and arrogance?

Conjure in your own mind an apparition of America and you will soon be surrounded by a host of spectral forms,[1] no single one of which is adequate to represent something as complex as our nation. On the other hand, however various those representations may be, they are likely to feature images of motion, talismans of travel—sailing ships that brought the first Europeans to these shores, cov-

This essay was written as part of a project led by Jose Ciprut, founder and director of "Cross-Campus Conversations at Penn," a University of Pennsylvania faculty colloquium exploring important issues in cross-disciplinary perspective.

ered wagons that took others across the continent, railroads span-
ning the land between the great oceans, automobiles on the open
road, airplanes in "the wild blue yonder," spaceships carrying astro-
nauts to explore the last frontier—suggesting not only the mobility
of Americans geographically and socially, but also the idea that
America is more about departures than arrivals, more about destina-
tions than the here and now, more about going there than being
there, more about hopes than memories. Whatever the goal is, we
agree that we are not yet there. We are still becoming.

Not only are we moving, but we are going in various directions at
the same time. Hints about the Idea of America are to be found in the
paradoxes that mark the frontlines of cultural conflict like the muzzle
flashes of opposing armies. We are materialistic, yet we are the most
religious people in the developed world. Our economic system is
proudly based upon selfishness, yet large-scale philanthropy was invented in America. We believe in the common man and disdain people
who put on airs of superiority, yet we are fascinated by celebrities.
Hard work is a cultural commandment, yet we are always looking for
get-rich-quick schemes. Our middle-class virtues stress delayed gratification, but we avail ourselves of instant coffee, fast foods, and quick
marriages. We are optimistic to a fault, but the jeremiad is a major
motif of our intellectual life. We admire the heroic perseverance of
championship athletes because they represent the triumph of individuals over great obstacles, so we set up a system to mass-produce
those exceptional individuals for Olympic competition. We are fa-
mously pragmatic, yet we are also the land of utopian experiments—
the largest of those experiments being the nation itself.

I am amused that the motif of the lonely hero, the unconstrained
individual, looms so large in the American imagination, from James
Fenimore Cooper's Natty Bumppo to the Hollywood heroes played
by John Wayne or Clint Eastwood. As powerful as that virile image of
splendid isolation is, the real genius of America is to be found in large-
scale organization: the transcontinental railroads, the great business
corporations, mammoth philanthropies, the effort to send men to the
moon and robots to Mars, not to mention the logistical efforts of World
War I, World War II, and currently of Operation Iraqi Freedom.

Something important about America is to be found in the conversations between opposing terms of a few binary opposites that lie at
the center of our being: liberalism and republicanism, individualism
and community, the One and the Many in the sense of our being one

nation and many cultures, and especially liberty and equality. That we used "freedom" as the name of our current effort in Iraq is a clue to the way we understand ourselves.

Freedom as National Purpose

Freedom is the most powerful word in the American vocabulary, centrally implicated in the meaning of America. (Foner 1998; Potter 1976; Wiebe 1995; Kammen 1986). Freedom's alter ego, liberty, is prominently present in the Declaration of Independence. The Preamble to the Constitution asserts that securing its blessings for ourselves and our posterity is a major purpose of government. When President Thomas Jefferson two hundred years ago sent Meriwether Lewis and William Clark to explore the Louisiana Purchase, he called the vast acquisition an "Empire for Liberty." Our patriotic songs invoke the nation as "sweet land of liberty." We pledge allegiance to the flag as the symbol of a republic devoted to "liberty and justice for all." When our leaders want to summon up "the better angels of our nature," freedom is usually there. President Abraham Lincoln when dedicating the military cemetery at Gettysburg in 1863, hoped that the Civil War would lead to a "new birth of freedom." Woodrow Wilson called his program of reform the "New Freedom." Franklin Delano Roosevelt invested World War II with transcendent significance by enunciating four freedoms as global goals: freedom of speech, freedom of religion, freedom from fear, and freedom from want. Martin Luther King, Jr. in 1963 at the March on Washington, had a dream of an America that would truly "let freedom ring" because in that America all God's children would be reconciled and therefore would be able to proclaim, "Free at last! Free at last! Thank God almighty, we are free at last!"

Problems begin to arise only when we pause to wonder what "freedom" means, and who is included in its embrace? As Isaiah Berlin noted, "Almost every moralist in human history has praised freedom. Like happiness and goodness, like nature and reality, it is a term whose meaning is so porous that there is little interpretation that it seems able to resist." Freedom has meant different things at different times and places, and it has meant different things to different people at the same time and place. Scholars have identified more than two hundred different meanings of freedom (Berlin, 2002: 168). That doesn't include Janet Joplin's definition: "Freedom's just another word for nothing left to lose."

Freedom for the Group

For the Puritans in seventeenth-century New England, freedom in the first instance was the ability of their communities to establish a society that was in accord with their understanding of the Bible, the kind of Biblical commonwealth they were not permitted to create in Great Britain, where the King was the Defender of the Faith and the Church of England was the established church. The first kind of freedom for them belonged to the group. As they proved over and over, it certainly did not imply religious toleration for other groups within the Massachusetts Bay Colony. Nor did it imply the absence of communal supervision of individual behavior and belief.

For individuals, what was offered was freedom from enslavement to sin, which freedom was to be achieved by strict conformity to the will of church and community. As the long-time leader of Massachusetts Bay, John Winthrop, put it in his speech to the General Court in 1645, "On Liberty," moral liberty is to be understood in terms of the covenant between God and man, and it is the "liberty to that only which is good, just, and honest.... This liberty is maintained and exercised in a way of subjection to authority; it is the same kind of liberty wherewith Christ hath made us free" (Kammen 2001: 20).

Colonial America, in general, was not devoted to religious toleration. Anglicans in Virginia had very different religious ideas from the Puritans in New England, but they agreed completely about the need of the society for uniformity of worship. Yet, by the time of the making of the Constitution in 1787, religious toleration was no longer a controversial subject. Freedom of religion is announced in two critical clauses of the First Amendment, adopted in 1789, though part of the motivation was to reassure the states which still relied on established churches that the federal government would not intervene. In the realm of ideas and values, few things are simple or simply straightforward.

Freedom from Bondage

Something of the explanation for the historic progression from uniformity to toleration is suggested by the experience of the State of Pennsylvania. In 1689, after the Glorious Revolution of 1688 that brought Mary, the Protestant daughter of James II, and her husband, William of Orange, to the throne, Parliament passed the Act of Toleration, which allowed nonconformists to worship without breaking the law, though atheists, Jews and Catholics could not vote or hold public office. The English had grown weary of killing and persecuting each other, to determine who could prescribe the mode of worship, and to exercise other aspects of sovereignty.

During the Commonwealth period (1649-60), Independents and orthodox Anglicans had made common cause to demand toleration from Oliver Cromwell's Puritan government. William Penn and the Quakers were shaped in their thinking about church-state relations by their experience during the Commonwealth period. The Quakers aligned themselves with the Independents, and in favor of religious toleration.

William Penn originally had been confirmed in the Anglican Church, but he became a Quaker in 1667 at the age of twenty-three. He was a zealous convert and was repeatedly arrested for preaching in public, which was considered to be incitement to riot. On one such occasion, in 1670, the jury found him not guilty, an early case of what we might now call "jury nullification." The judge sent him to jail anyway. In fact, the judge sent the jury to jail as well. However, a higher court reversed these rulings and set William Penn free.

While in jail on this occasion, Penn wrote a tract, "The Great Cause of Liberty of Conscience," in which he argued in favor of freedom of worship. Consequently, Penn founded his colony in 1682 explicitly on the theory of religious liberty for all who professed a belief in a supreme being, though Jews could not vote or hold office, nor could Africans or Indians, and atheists were not knowingly allowed residence.

Despite the toleration, even William Penn thought that government was a religious undertaking. Pennsylvania was thus a "Holy Experiment," and the sorts of personal behavior that would draw God's wrath (swearing, cursing, lying, profane talking, drunkenness, whoredom, etc.) were against the law. On the other hand, Penn also believed that, "Force can make a hypocrite, but only faith can make a Christian." Consequently, his proprietary colony was to be a refuge for Quakers and other victims of religious persecution— though there were limits on who was included in the freedom of self-governance.

A representative assembly, required by Penn's charter from Charles II, existed from the start, as well as a council whose members were appointed by the Proprietor. In the Preface to the Frame of Government of 1682, Penn wrote that there is a truth that is shared by Monarchy, Oligarchy, and Democracy: "Any Government is Free to the People under it (what-ever be the Frame) where the Laws Rule, and the People are a Party to those Laws, and more than this is Tyranny, Oligarchy or Confusion.... For Liberty without Obedience is Confusion, and Obedience without Liberty is Slavery" (Dunn and Dunn, 1982: 213-14).

In 1701, after years of bickering about the powers of the Assembly, Penn yielded, abolished the appointive Council, and issued a "Charter of Liberties." It was interchangeably called the "Charter of Privileges," revealing the unspoken assumption of the time that rights were privileges that were granted by one's superiors in the great hierarchy descending from the sovereign monarch. The Charter of 1701 established a unicameral legislature with substantially enhanced powers of local self-government. Henceforth, an elected unicameral legislature and a Governor appointed by the Proprietor ruled over the colony. In 1705, with Queen Anne on the throne, Parliament forced the colony to apply the Test Oath to office holders, thus prohibiting Catholics as well as Jews and nonbelievers from holding office.

In 1751, the first jubilee of the Charter of Liberties of 1701, the Assembly commissioned a bell to be struck. It was to hang in the statehouse in Philadelphia, and to be rung on important ceremonial occasions. The speaker of the assembly ordered an inscription to be engraved on the bell. It was from Leviticus 25: 10: "Proclaim LIBERTY throughout all the land unto all the inhabitants thereof." The liberty that the Speaker and the Assembly had in mind was the liberty of "freemen" to participate in the making of the laws under which they were to live. It was the "home rule" nature of the Charter of Privileges that was being celebrated.

The inscription from Leviticus is a commandment through Moses from God to honor Jubilee, which was to be celebrated after a week of Sabbath years, or every fiftieth year. In the year of Jubilee, believers are to free their slaves and to forgive their debts. Jubilee thus was about freedom, but not about freedom from the tyranny of government. It was about freedom from men oppressing each other. It was also about duty. This takes us back to the most prevalent notion of liberty in the colonial period: freedom from sin, which is obtained by perfect obedience to the Word of God.

Nevertheless, the protean word "Freedom" was inscribed on the Bell. It was rung in Philadelphia in 1776, to announce the Declaration of Independence—a document that commenced the struggle of the colonists for freedom in the sense of "home rule" but that also initiated a quest that has continuously discovered new meanings of liberty. Most important, the Declaration and the Constitution located sovereignty in the people; no longer would rights and liberties be viewed as privileges that flowed down from above, granted by Kings or Lords. The Declaration also proclaimed the radical notion that "all men are born equal, that they are endowed by their Creator with certain unalienable Rights, that among these are Life, Liberty, and the pursuit of Happiness."

It was this universal but unrealized promise of freedom that abolitionists picked up in the 1830s. They began using the Bell as the symbol of their effort to abolish human slavery and began referring to it as the Liberty Bell.

Freedom as Self-Reliance

In the course of the eighteenth century, several varieties of freedom were at play in Colonial America. Republican theory, deployed by British dissenters, emphasized that the source of authority was to be found in the citizens. Everyone was subject to the law, but subjects were to participate in the making of the laws. Since one didn't want laws that served the interests of a particular person or faction, it was important that the representatives of the people be citizens of great virtue, and virtue was to be found among those who were independent enough to discern the common interest and to resist the pressures of self-interested individuals and factions. In short, virtue was to be found among gentlemen of property and standing. Without property, a man was dependent on others, and thus not fully free.[2] At the time of the Revolution, most colonists were un-free in the sense that they were dependent upon someone, usually the patriarchal head of a household: women, children, apprentices, indentured servants, and slaves. Property, argued John Locke in "The Second Treatise of Government," was the guarantor of freedom. "Man being born, as has been proved, with a Title to perfect Freedom, and an uncontrolled enjoyment of all the Rights and Privileges of the Law of Nature, equally with any other Man, or number of men in the world, hath by Nature a Power, not only to preserve his Property, that is, his Life, Liberty and Estate, against the Inquiries and Attempts of other Men; but to judge of, and punish the breaches of that Law in others" (quoted in Gerber, 2002: 229).

The First Great Awakening, exciting the colonies in the mid-years of the eighteenth century, emphasized the direct and personal relationship between the individual and God, which one might see as the beginnings of theological individualism. At the same time, the great free market revolution was also causing people to begin to conceive of freedom in individualistic, as opposed to communal, terms. With the free market as the model, the new vision was that a just society should not depend on the republican ideal of leaders with sufficient virtue, authorized to choose policies that would serve the general interest of society as a whole. A just society more reliably was the product of the automatic balancing that would occur if every individual pursued his own self-interest. Indeed, in liberal theory, there is no such thing as the "general interest." After the Revolution, and then rapidly in the nineteenth century as immigration, industrialization, and urbanization continued to transform America, individualism, understood as self-reliance, became the dominant mindset of America. (Appleby 1992a; Sandel 1998; Shain 1994).

Not surprisingly, the tycoons of the Gilded Age who built the modern industrial and financial corporations, and amassed the great American fortunes, found this notion of self-reliance very attractive, even flattering, especially when combined with the then fashionable Darwinian idea of the survival of the fittest. When confronting labor unions, conservatives used the liberal argument that each worker had "freedom of contract," which is to say that the union ought not to interfere with the worker's right to sell his labor to the employer. Progressives responded with a new view of freedom that recognized that individuals could be as oppressed by other human beings as they could be by government—and especially so by these new aggregations of economic power. The progressive notion was that the government should be used as the democratic balance wheel of justice, regulating the free market and providing those things, such as education, that would allow the individual to have a chance to realize his full potential. From the late nineteenth century to this day, the role of government has been at the center of political conflict in the United States.

Meanwhile, back in the eighteenth century, our Revolution was fought to protect the old British notion of freedom as being the right of "freemen" to participate in making the laws under which everyone would live. If the king and Parliament insisted on taxation without representation, then perhaps liberty could only be found when the colonies were free from the control of the Empire. In the process of explaining themselves to the world, and of rallying support among the American colonial population, the Founding Fathers chose to resort to "natural rights" philosophy, and to use the concepts of "liberty" and "equality," which contained a powerful capacity to grow, to include more and more people in their protective embrace, and slowly to reduce the conflicts between the theory and practice of freedom.

From Subjects to Citizens

With "liberty" and "equality" joined together by the founding documents[3], it was natural that Americans during the Revolution would shift from referring to themselves as "subjects" of the crown to seeing themselves as "citizens" of the United States of America. Citizenship has an equalizing aspect to it. The rights and privileges of citizenship are enjoyed equally by all, are they not? Actually, the Constitution was originally silent on the question of what the precise "privileges and immunities" of citizenship were, and on the matter of who is a citizen and who is not. The assumption of the government was that every free person who did not flee the country during the Revolution was a citizen (Smith 1997).

Women occupied a particularly anomalous place inasmuch as their status generally followed that of their father or husband, the male head-of–household on whom they were dependent. Widows and spinsters with property were in most matters exceptions because they were independent. They could not vote, however, until the Nineteenth Amendment was ratified in 1920. Indians also occupied an ambiguous position until they were specifically declared to be citizens by act of Congress in 1934 (Kerber 1997).

A further hint that Americans had a racialized notion of national identity came in the Naturalization Act of 1790, which restricted eligibility for naturalization to "free white persons." This restriction was not changed until the McCarren–Walter Act of 1952, though that act left in place the "national origins quota" system that was itself the public policy embodiment of a racialized notion of the American identity.[4]

Free blacks were not as free as free whites, a fact confirmed by countless discriminations suffered by people of color in non-slave states in the antebellum period. Then, in the infamous *Dred Scott* decision in 1857, Chief Judge Roger B. Taney wrote for the majority of the Supreme Court that people of African descent were not citizens of the United States and did not enjoy the "rights of privileges of citizenship."

The Fourteenth Amendment, ratified in 1868, was the second of the three great Civil War Amendments. It voided *Dred Scott* and created a national citizenship, along with state citizenship, and declared that all "persons" had a right to the "equal protection of the law." Though violated in letter and spirit, this provision, over time, has been a powerful tool in the development of a more inclusive and tolerant society. In that atmosphere, in 1870, the Naturalization Act of 1790 was amended to allow the naturalization of African immigrants.

Thousands of Chinese came to the United States in the 1840s and 1850s, mostly to the West Coast and to work on the transcontinental railroads. They were not eligible for naturalization, though their children born in the U.S. were automatically citizens. The Chinese Exclusion Act in 1882 wrote into immigration law the prejudices of European Americans: It barred Chinese laborers. During World War II, the Chinese were allies. Congress repealed this insulting restriction, leaving Chinese immigration to be governed by the national origins system, under which China's quota for 1943 was 105 people.

Japanese started coming to the United States in significant numbers in the 1890s and in the first decade of the twentieth century, stirring up the same sort of anti-Asian sentiment. The result was the Gentlemen's Agreement of 1900, in which the United States promised not to exclude Japanese by statute if Japan drastically limited the emigration of laborers. This arrangement was made stronger and more explicit through a series of diplomatic notes in 1907 and in 1908. The racial assumptions of this policy became apparent in particularly ugly form during World War II when the U.S. government interned thousands of Japanese-American citizens, as well as Japanese aliens, while placing German aliens under a very loose monitoring system.

Meanwhile, after the Civil War, during the 1880s and after, the magnitude and character of European immigration changed, increasing dramatically and shifting from northern and western Europe to eastern and southern Europe. The "New Immigration" stimulated a vigorous immigration restriction movement, as well as aggressive cultural assimilation efforts. While in principle and in effect, immigration policy remained open to all Europeans, in practice the more

one could look like and act like an Anglo-American, the more welcome one was.

World War I interrupted the flow of these "huddled masses yearn-
ing to breathe free," as they were described in the idealistic lines of
the poem by Emma Lazarus (1849-1887) and inscribed on the base
of the Statue of Liberty in 1903. Following the Great War, in step
with the growing isolationism of the time, the immigration restriction movement was successful in getting the Congress to pass the
National Origins Quota Act of 1921, amended in 1924. The new
policy set a low limit on overall annual immigration (350,000 per
year at the beginning, as compared to almost one million per year in
the first decade of the century) and provided that the quota be allo-
cated to countries based on their proportion of the U.S. population
in 1890. This was intended to freeze the ethnic character of the
American population at its 1890 composition.

First the Great Depression and then World War II limited the flow
of immigrants to a trickle, even fewer than the official quota, but the
National Origins Quota system remained in effect until it was replaced in 1965 by a new immigration law that was in tune with the
newly ascendant racial egalitarianism. Since that revolutionary act,
increasing numbers of Hispanic and Asian immigrants have found
their way into the United States, giving rise to struggles over the
meanings of the multiculturalism that increasingly is the reality of
American life. Racial nationalism, dominant from the Revolution to
the 1960s, had been replaced by civic nationalism, under whose
dispensation we currently live.

Individualism and Community

When the French aristocrat, Alexis de Tocqueville, visited the
United States during Andrew Jackson's presidency, he entitled his
brilliant analysis of the society he found there *Democracy in America*.
First published in 1835, it is so full of deep insights that the America
it describes is still recognizable almost two centuries later. Tocqueville
was not always right, of course. For instance, he thought the passion
of Americans for equality would always win out in the competition
with liberty, yet the U.S. today has the greatest internal disparity of
wealth and income among the industrialized nations.

On the other hand, Tocqueville did see many things clearly. In
particular, he saw the reciprocal relationship between individualism
and community. He coined the term "individualism" to describe the

self-reliance and self-rule that he found in America, and he worried about it, as you might expect a European aristocrat to do: "Thus not only does democracy make each man forget his ancestors, but it hides his descendants from him and separates him from his contemporaries; it constantly leads him back toward himself alone and threatens finally to confine him wholly in the solitude of his own heart. (Tocqueville, 2000/II: 484).

Yet, Tocqueville also noticed that Americans are a "nation of joiners," as Arthur Schlesinger, Sr. has termed it—a society in which voluntary associations are a way of life: "Americans of all ages, all conditions, all minds constantly unite. Not only do they also have commercial and industrial associations, in which all take part, but they also have associations of a thousand other kinds: religious, moral, grave, futile, very general and very particular, immense and very small; Americans use associations to give fetes, to found seminaries, to build inns, to raise churches, to distribute books, to send missionaries to the antipodes; in this manner they create hospitals, prisons, schools. Finally, if it is a question of bringing to light a truth or developing a sentiment with the support of a great example, they associate. Everywhere that, at the head of a new undertaking, you see the government in France and a great lord in England, count on it that you will perceive an association in the United States" (Tocqueville, 2000/II: 489).

This dialogic relationship between individualism and community is one of the main themes of American history. It is not really a tension because Americans in public opinion polls express the same level of enthusiasm for the notion of individualism as for community. Yet it seems paradoxical that we live utterly alone, but have no meaning, no identity, apart from the social context in which we are embedded. It is this two-ness in our natures that makes us long for "community." The connection, as Gordon Wood has argued (1993: 220), is that "social love" derives from "self-love." As Robert Wiebe suggests (1995: 40), "Free individuals formed democratic communities [and] democratic communities sustained free individuals." Americans continue to live their lives in this conversation between individualism and community.

Creating a National Sentiment

Meanwhile, the young United States had to create a sense of nationhood that other nations inherited. Living as they did in local communities and separate colonies, without any collective memory other than the heroic struggle for independence, ordinary citizens had little idea of what it meant to be an American. George Washington, speaking the words written by Alexander Hamilton, noted in his Farewell Address that Americans needed to develop a "national sentiment" if they were to survive as a nation in the family of nations. What was that sentiment to be? He did not say.

European intellectuals had always seen the New World as a place where one or one's group could escape the corruptions and restrictions of European society and build a society that would avoid or correct all of the perceived problems of Europe. Alternatively, the colonies were seen simply as the land of opportunity, of second chances, or of first chances for second sons—a place open to talent and industry. America served as a projection of European dreams and nightmares.

It is not surprising, therefore, that the "national sentiment" in the late eighteenth century came from the "party of hope" in Europe. Joyce Appleby finds the seeds of American "exceptionalism" in the way European intellectuals viewed the newly founded United States. She quotes a French progressive as saying of the United States "They are the hope of the human race; they may well become its model." Denis Diderot called the new republic an asylum from fanaticism and tyranny "for all the peoples of Europe," and Thomas Jefferson's secretary, still in France after Jefferson's return home, compared Americans to a group of prisoners who have broken out of a "common gaol" (i.e., Europe) and are being watched by their fellow inmates with "an anxious eye" to see if they make good their escape. Bernard Fay, the French historian, wrote later that "not a book on America was printed between 1775 and 1790 but ended with a sort of homily on America as the future of mankind" (Appleby, 1992b: 419). To European dissidents of all kinds, the United States represented the possibility of social reform. In a sense, Americans learned who they were from these Europeans, who were using America to their own rhetorical ends (Appleby 2000, Woodward 991, Greene 1993).

These reveries of Europeans were popular in the United States because they offered eighteenth-century Americans a collective identity before they had any other basis for spiritual unity. As the politics of the 1790s grew more heated, the "exceptionalism" that was latent in colonial experience was reformulated into a specific destiny for the nation, a destiny that was tied to European dreams as well as to the political principles enunciated in the Declaration and the Constitution, as ambiguous as those were. This was the beginning of the conscious conception of American "exceptionalism"—the making of a new "imagined community" that forms the nation. The United States was in reality an insignificant country. In the American imagination, however, the nation became the vanguard of human progress, the very exemplar of liberty—"the last best hope on earth," as Lincoln said.

This Grand Narrative of American history has been under attack for the past two generations as being triumphalist and Eurocentric, which is to say, oblivious to the gaps between creed and reality, forgetful of the bitter conflicts among Americans, that have offered alternative outcomes for America at every step along the way. One can think of realities that are at odds with the innocence of our myth: slavery, the genocide of Native Americans, anti-Catholicism, nativism, anti-Semitism, xenophobia, anti-Asian feelings, the exploitation of "wage slaves," adventures in imperialism, and the repression of dissidents during the Red Scare in 1919-20 at the time of the Russian Revolution or during the McCarthyism of the 1950s. Nevertheless, we are still inspired by our commitment to the Revolutionary ideals of liberty and equality, even as we continue to try to understand their meaning.

The most obvious example of a disjunction between theory and practice, of course, was human slavery. A number of the signers of the Declaration and drafters of the Constitution were slave owners. Even though an abolitionist movement already existed, the Constitution tacitly recognized slavery in order to bind the slave states to the Union. Besides, at the time of the making of the Constitution, many expected slavery to die of its own inefficiency. The invention of the cotton gin and the steamboat, however, breathed new profits into the corpse.

The argument over human slavery, in a country devoted to human freedom, intensified during the debates that led to the Missouri Compromise in 1820. It posed a moral question that was increasingly difficult to avoid. Finally, the election of Abraham Lincoln in 1860 was taken by white southerners to convey a signal that the national government was in the hands of forces hostile to their "peculiar institution," the popular euphemism for slavery. Eleven of the fifteen slave states decided to leave the union.

And the war came. Though initially the North fought simply "to preserve the Union," it is clear that the reason for war having been slavery, freedom from human bondage became the meaning of the war. Concluding that the federal government in the hands of Republicans threatened the institution of slavery, the South seceded to protect the freedom of states and local communities to determine their own social arrangements. The Civil War in this sense was a contest between two opposing ideas of freedom (Foner 1988: 95, McPherson 1988: vii).

The Civil War settled the question of chattel slavery, but Reconstruction did not settle the question of what "freedom" would mean for the former slaves. By 1877, the white South and the white North were reconciled at the expense of African Americans, who were abandoned—their second-class citizenship was to be defined by white Southerners in legally prescribed segregation and through political disfranchisement, a system of racial subordination put into place in the twenty years that would follow 1890, the year of the Mississippi Constitutional Convention, held to curb black voter participation by seemingly legitimate means, such as the imposition of a literacy test.

The long struggle by African Americans and their allies, toward achieving equal citizenship, produced notable victories in the first half of the twentieth century, albeit no dramatic change in racial discrimination. Then, under the slogan of "Freedom Now," the civil rights movement of the 1950s and 1960s, together with the other social justice movements that it inspired, led to the erasure of legally prescribed discrimination from the statute books, fostering a shift toward cultural diversity and social inclusiveness, with equal rights and opportunities for all.

Parallel to the efforts in the 1960s of previously marginalized groups (blacks, American Indians, women, Hispanics, gays, lesbians, and people with disabilities) to overcome the hitherto oppressive external roadblocks to individual achievement was the effort of the counterculture to free individuals from equally oppressive internal roadblocks posed by cultural constraints. "If it feels good, do it," was the mantra. The counterculture ridiculed every middle-class tenet: hard work as its own reward, postponement of gratification, self-control, responsibility for family and community, and so on. What the counterculture was asserting was that it was not enough to strive for a society in which everyone could become whatever they wanted to become. We should create a society in which people were free to want to be whatever kind of person they could imagine being. This raises an interesting question about the "freely choosing autonomous self" of liberal theory: who is the "real" self that is doing the "wanting," the "imagining," and the "choosing"? And is that real "self" free of oppressive cultural commandments?[5]

Freedom as Self-Invention

This invocation of the liberty of self-invention did not begin with the counterculture, and surely not with singer-actress Madonna's multiple personalities. As an early self-fabricator, Benjamin Franklin comes to mind. Perhaps the story of Frederick Douglass can illustrate this dimension of the malleability of freedom.

Douglass was born a slave on a Maryland plantation. At the age of about eight, sent to Baltimore to live with a family there, he had a transforming experience, which he described in the first of his three autobiographies, written at different points in his long life: "Very soon after I went to live with Mr. and Mrs. Auld, she very kindly commenced to teach me the abc. After I had learned this she assisted me in learning to spell words of three or four letters. Just at this point of my progress, Mr. Auld found out what was going on, and at once forbade Mrs. Auld to instruct me further, telling her, among other things, that it was unlawful, as well as unsafe, to teach a slave to read. To use his own words further, he said, if you give a nigger an inch he will take a mile. A nigger should know nothing but to obey his master; to do as he is told to do. Learning would spoil the best nigger in the world. Now, said he, if they teach that nigger (speaking of myself) how to read, there would be no keeping him. It would forever unfit him to be a slave. He would at once become unmanageable and of no value to his master. As to himself it could do him no good but a great deal of harm. It would make him discontented and unhappy.... These words sank deep into my heart, stirred up sentiments within that lay slumbering and called into existence an entirely new train of thought. It was a new, a special revelation explaining dark and mysterious things with which my youthful understanding had struggled in vain. I now understood what had been, to me, a most perplexing difficulty; to wit, the white man's power to enslave the black man. It was a grand achievement, and I prized it highly. From that moment I understood the pathway from slavery to freedom. (Douglass 1993: 57-58).

Mr. Auld was right. Though Mrs. Auld ceased to teach her young slave, Douglass continued to learn on his own. Soon, he escaped to New York. From that point of physical emancipation, he started the process of becoming the Frederick Douglass that we know. This story of self-liberation through learning has two meanings: He left physically and escaped chattel slavery. Then he exercised his liberty to make himself into the kind of free man that he wanted to be.

I believe that when Frederick Douglass composed this first self-presentation in 1845 at the age of twenty-seven, he knew exactly what he was doing. He knew that he was creating a persona. He was not only creating himself, but he was portraying someone in print. I infer that from the way *The Narrative* is written, but also because Douglass was writing fairly soon after William Ellery Channing published a widely read book, in 1837, entitled *Self-Culture*—a set of lectures that he had been giving to working-class audiences. Channing was preaching not the virtue of rags-to-riches (that would come later, in the 103 novels and books for juveniles to be written by Horatio Alger in the last third of the nineteenth century); he was preaching the virtue of the self-made man in its original sense: how to master oneself, build character, and lead a moral life.

The liberty of self-invention is a characteristically American phenomenon, reflected in the power of the myth of the frontier; recognizable in our therapeutic culture; in television programs such as *Extreme Makeover* that, however superficially, trade upon our desire to start anew; in the consumer culture that invites us to buy at the store the identity that we want; in our commitment to second chances; and even in our religious desire to be "born again."

Liberty Ordered and Balanced

All of this is to say that, historically, we have argued over what liberty means and who should enjoy its blessings. Those struggles were made inevitable by the very fact that liberty has been at the core of our self-image from the birth of the nation to the present. A prize so precious is bound to attract suitors and protectors, both noble and profane.

We have therefore thought of liberty as freedom from sin, the kind of freedom which is to be achieved through perfect obedience to some authority's interpretation of God's word; personal independence, which can be secured by owning property; freedom from chattel slavery, the absence of wage slavery; the ability to reinvent

oneself; freedom from discrimination because of one's group identity; participation in self-governance; religious toleration; local self-
government; and countless other definitions.

As a society, we have learned how to hold in dynamic tension the
notion that liberty has to do with the absence of governmental constraints and the Progressive Era idea that, in a complex and intercon-
nected economy, with vast powers over the individual wielded by
invisible forces and distant people, the government must act in positive ways that should help the individual to free himself and to achieve
self-realization.

A constant theme throughout has been the need for "ordered liberty":

> America the beautiful
> God shed his grace on thee.
> Confirm thy soul in self control,
> Thy liberty in law.[6]

Or, as the eminent jurist Learned Hand put it in 1944 in his address, "The Spirit of Liberty," when addressing the question, "What
is liberty?": "It is not the ruthless, the unbridled will; it is not freedom to do as one likes. That is the denial of liberty, and leads straight
to its overthrow. A society in which men recognize no check upon
their freedom soon becomes a society where freedom is the posses-
sion of only a savage few (Kammen 2001: 171).

Several years ago the billionaire financier, George Soros, who is
active in encouraging the growth of capitalism and democracy in
the countries of the former Soviet Union, wrote that unregulated
free markets do not breed democracy; they breed thugs (Soros 1997).
In a similar vein, though somewhat more elegantly, the historian of
ideas, Isaiah Berlin, wrote, "Both liberty and equality are among the
primary goals pursued by human beings through many centuries;
but total liberty for wolves is death to the lambs, total liberty of the
powerful, the gifted, is not compatible with the rights to a decent
existence of the weak and the less gifted" (Berlin 1990: 12).

A constant worry through these centuries of freedom is that it
would degrade into some form of uncivilized society. Thus eighteenth-century commentators worried that liberty would undermine
the authority that they assumed was necessary to keep order. Theodore
Adorno and other social scientists of the twentieth century, who were
trying to explain totalitarianism, theorized that freedom breeds such

feelings of insecurity and anxiety that many ("authoritarian person-alities") will seek security in submission to some strong authority. In two hundred years, the American people progressed from worrying that too much freedom would lead to anarchic disorder to fearing that too much freedom would lead to regimentation.

It is both wonderful and worrisome that freedom is so variegated in its meanings and so powerful in its appeal. It tells us who we are and reminds us of whom we must not become. It gives Americans a standard by which we can measure the worth of proposed policies, and it allows our leaders to mobilize support for actions that require sacrifice but that will be beneficial in the long run. At the same time, it also allows our leaders to mask less altruistic motives, to lead us in directions in which we should not be going. The task of the citizen is to discern the difference between those two rhetorical uses of the idea of freedom. It depends on an alert and healthy democracy. If citizens fail in that task, freedom will fail.

Liberty, in short, is a communal enterprise. Whatever it means, whether it is the absence of governmental or social intrusion into the space in which the individual is autonomous (freedom *from*....), or the availability of governmental and social support to overcome barriers like poverty or ignorance (freedom *to*....), it depends on the active commitment of the members of the society. If liberty is not cherished and nurtured by the community to which we belong, so that it is expressed in the laws that apply to everyone equally, and if it does not include all citizens alike, it will soon not exist for any but the fiercest animals in the urbanized jungle. Furthermore, since lib-erty changes its meaning from time to time, and place to place, it will always be unfinished and contingent—forever in need of being remolded by our very selves, to defend against new threats but also to take advantage of new opportunities for each civic participant.

Notes

1. See *Talk To Me*, a documentary film by Andrea Simon, Arcadia Pictures, New York, NY.
2. See John J. Mulhern (forthcoming) "The Political Economy of Citizenship," in Jose V. Ciprut, editor, *The Future of Citizenship.*
3. For a discussion of the democratic dilemma created by these two terms, see Mark Gaige (forthcoming), "Citizen: Past Practices, Prospective Patterns," in Jose V. Ciprut, editor, *The Future of Citizenship.*
4. There were, and are, three ways to obtain American citizenship: being born in the U.S. (*jus soli*); being born of American parents (*jus sanguine*); and being naturalized.
5. For a detailed account, see David R. Williams, "Ego and Ethos" (forthcoming), in Jose V. Ciprut, editor, *Ethics: A Multidisciplinary Re-Examination.*

6.   Words by Katherine Lee Bates, a professor at Wellesley College, written during a trip to Colorado, 1893.

References

Appleby, Joyce. 1992a. *Liberalism and Republicanism in the Historical Imagination.* Cambridge, MA: Harvard University Press.

_____.1992b. "Recovering America's Historic Diversity: Beyond Exceptionalism." *Journal of American History*, September 1992, pp. 419-431.

_____. 2000. *Inheriting the Revolution: The First Generation of Americans.* Cambridge. MA: Harvard University Press.

Berlin, Isaiah. 2002. "Two Concepts of Liberty," in Henry Hardy, ed., *Liberty*. New York and Oxford: Oxford University Press.

_____. 1990. "The Pursuit of the Ideal," in Henry Hardy, ed., *The Crooked Timber of Humanity*, London: John Murray (Publishers) Ltd.

Douglass, Frederick. 1993. *Narrative of the Life of Frederick Douglass, An American Slave, Written by Himself*, edited and with an introduction by David Blight. Boston: Bedford Books of St. Martin's Press.

Dunn, Richard and Mary Maples Dunn, eds. 1982. *The Papers of William Penn*, vol. 2, 1680-1684. Philadelphia: University of Pennsylvania Press.

Foner, Eric.1998. *The Story of American Freedom*. New York: W.W. Norton and Company.

Gerber, Scott Douglas, ed. 2002. *The Declaration of Independence: Origins and Impact*, Washington, DC: CQ   Press.

Greene, Jack P. 1993. *The Intellectual Construction of America: Exceptionalism and Identity From 1492 to 1800.* Chapel Hill: The University of North Carolina Press.

Kammen, Michael. 2001. *Spheres of Liberty: Changing Perceptions of Liberty in American Culture.* Jackson: University Press of Mississippi, 2001. First published in 1986 by the University of Wisconsin Press.

Kerber, Linda. 1997. "The Meanings of Citizenship." *Journal of American History*. December 1997, pp. 833-854.

McPherson, James M. 1988. *Battle Cry of Freedom.* New York: Ballantine Books.

Potter, David. 1976. *Freedom and Its Limitations in American Life*. Stanford, CA: Stanford University Press.

Sandel, Michael. 1998. *Liberalism and the Limits of Justice*, second edition. Cambridge, UK: Cambridge University Press.

Shain, Barry Alan. 1994. *The Myth of American Individualism: The Protestant Origins of American Political Thought*, Princeton, NJ: Princeton University Press.

Smith, Rogers. 1997. *Civic Ideals: Conflicting Visions of Citizenship in U.S. History*. New Haven, CT: Yale University Press.

Soros, George. 1997. "The Capitalist Threat." *Atlantic Monthly* (Feb. 1997). Also available at: http: //www.theatlantic.com/issues/97feb/capital/capital.htm

Tocqueville, Alexis de. 2000. *Democracy in America*, edited by Harvey Mansfield and Delba Winthrop. Chicago: University of Chicago Press.

Wiebe, Robert. 1995. *Self-Rule: A Cultural History of American Democracy.* Chicago: University of Chicago Press.

Wood, Gordon. 1993. *The Radicalness of the American Revolution.* New York: Vintage Books of Random House, Inc. Originally published by Alfred A. Knopf, Inc., 1993.

Woodward, C. Vann. 1991. *The Old World's New World.* New York: Oxford University Press.

Index

143